The Essential Guide

for

Hiring

&

Getting Hired

Lou Adler

the essential guide for

Hiring
& Getting Hired

ISBN 978-0-9889574-1-1 (print edition)
ISBN 978-0-9889574-0-4 (e-book)

*THIS BOOK IS FIRST DEDICATED TO EVERY PERSON
WHO WANTS TO GET THE JOB THEY DESERVE.*

*IT'S ALSO DEDICATED TO EVERY HIRING MANAGER
WHO'S EVER MADE A HIRING MISTAKE.*

Contents

Introduction & Organization of the Book

I've been in the recruiting industry for almost 35 years and counting. Before that, I had a pretty good run at two major Fortune 500 companies. Over the years I learned some big lessons and some great tactics about hiring top talent. All of the best ones are included here, or by reference to my earlier book, *Hire With Your Head* (©2007. Third Edition. John Wiley and Sons, Inc.). Hire With Your Head was written for hiring managers and recruiters with the focus on finding great candidates, interviewing and assessing them, and negotiating offers on fair and equitable terms. This book has been written for anyone involved in any aspect of the hiring process. This includes candidates, people who aren't looking but will be or should be, anyone who needs to interview anyone else, and of course hiring managers, recruiters, and company executives who care about hiring great people.

Since the first edition of *Hire With Your Head* was written in 1997, much has changed, but not as much as you might think. The job boards have come and gone and come again. Social networks have emerged as the new standard for finding people and finding jobs. The workforce has been globalized. Corporate recruiters have become an industry force and external search firms now play a different, but still critical role. New analytical tools have emerged, including supply vs.

demand analysis and real-time recruiter dashboards tracking every measure of ongoing performance.

Yet not much is really different. Few hiring managers are fully engaged in what is often called their most important task. Companies still post boring job descriptions hoping to find a person who has both an economic need to apply and is also a top performer. We still use indirect measures to assess candidates. Few recruiters are considered true partners and coaches by their hiring manager clients, just as they were pre-Internet. Most surprising of all is that most companies still spend most of their resources and efforts targeting the 17% of candidates who are actively looking, yet all want to hire the 83% who aren't.[1]

Here's my take on why not much has changed:

1) Companies continue to seek out the next sourcing silver bullet, expecting a bunch of top people to be actively looking in some secret place no one else has been able to find.

2) Companies continue to rely on a "surplus of candidates" mentality when designing their hiring processes. The problem is that you can't use a surplus approach in a talent scarcity situation.

3) While hiring top talent is good corporate-speak, it doesn't translate down to the operating level where hiring decisions are made. If it did, hiring managers' primary performance measure would be the quality of the people on their team and whom they've hired.

4) Everyone makes excuses and no one takes responsibility for Quality of Hire. The legal and compensation groups are blamed for just about everything, but too much work, disengaged managers, and silly bureaucratic rules represent the balance.

---

1 Joint Adler Group, Inc. and LinkedIn study 2011 (http://budurl.com/LIblog2)

5) Candidates don't know how to play the hiring game. Some are too eager, some not eager enough. Some talk too much, some not enough. Most don't know how to present themselves properly. Too many think maximizing compensation is more important than maximizing the career opportunity. All in all, it's not surprising that people take jobs for all of the wrong reasons, and wonder why they're not doing as well as they should be.

All of these issues will be addressed, dissected, understood, and reworked in a hands-on, practical way. There is not one idea in this book that has not been tried out multiple times, often hundreds, and in some cases thousands of times, by myself and many others. However, since the book has been written to appeal to multiple perspectives, here are some suggestions on how to get the most value from the ideas and solutions presented:

1) If you're a **candidate**, take advantage of the existing ill-designed systems and learn to navigate around the roadblocks and through the detours.

2) If you're a **recruiter**, work together with one of your hiring managers and learn how to find and hire one great person. You'll get the hang of it pretty quickly, and then you can start convincing all of your other hiring managers how hiring needs to be done.

3) If you're a **hiring manager**, find a recruiter you trust and work on your toughest new hiring project together. Then hone the process and coach your other managers through the techniques.

4) If you're a **recruiting or HR leader**, conduct a benchmark pilot program comparing the approaches mentioned in the book to your current processes. You'll quickly discover that when Quality of Hire is the primary or driving metric, quality improves, costs decline, and time-to-fill shortens.

5) If you're a **company executive**, understand why your talent acquisition strategy is sound in theory, but flawed in execution.

To get a sense of this, all you have to do is look at some of your company's public job postings. As you read them, ask yourself if a top fully employed person who is not looking would spend the time and energy to even consider them.

Google's Project Oxygen and Gallup's Q12

Everyone intuitively knows that hiring top talent should be one of the primary focuses of hiring managers. Surprisingly few managers are measured on how well they do, and most do it any way they want. Most make excuses of the "have to get the work done" variety as to why it's more talk and hope than reality.

Understanding why people perform at peak levels or underperform is not unknown science. What's surprising is that companies don't take this into account when hiring someone. Instead, they decide to fix the problem after the fact.

For example, in 2011 Google presented the results of an internal study referred to as Project Oxygen (http://budurl.com/agoxygen). The idea was to find out what it took to be a great manager at Google. Based on extensive employee reviews and satisfaction surveys it was clear that the importance of the job and the quality of the manager were critical drivers of performance. The New York Times interviewed Laszlo Bock, their Chief People Officer, about this study, which focused on what it took to be a great manager at Google. This minor quote says quite a lot:

> *But Mr. Bock's group found that technical expertise — the ability, say, to write computer code in your sleep — ranked dead last among Google's big eight. What employees valued most were even-keeled bosses who made time for one-on-one meetings, who helped people puzzle through problems by asking questions, not dictating answers, and who took an interest in employees' lives and careers.*

"In the Google context, we'd always believed that to be a manager, particularly on the engineering side, you need to be as deep or deeper a technical expert than the people who work for you," Mr. Bock says. "It turns out that that's absolutely the least important thing. It's important, but pales in comparison. Much more important is just making that connection and being accessible."[2]

In 1999 Marcus Buckingham and Curt Coffman of the Gallup Group wrote *First Break All the Rules: What the World's Greatest Managers Do Differently.* This is where they first introduced their Q12 list of criteria that employees require in order to maximize their performance and on-the-job satisfaction. At the top of the list were: clarifying expectations up front, providing people with the right tools and resources to do the job properly, having managers that support them, and being assigned work they enjoy and are good at. As part of the study, Buckingham and Coffman described four keys to becoming an excellent manager. These involved defining the results, finding people who could deliver these results, leveraging their employees' strengths, and selecting staff for talent, not raw knowledge or skills.

What's most surprising is that hiring managers, HR leaders, and company executives ignore all of this obvious stuff. The solution does not take a PhD or rocket science. Most hiring problems can be eliminated by making one fundamental and simple change – replacing job descriptions with a list of performance objectives the new hire is expected to achieve. Not knowing any better, I started doing this on the first day I became a recruiter. Over the next 20 years, and 1,500 placements later, less than five percent of these people were let go in the first year. Even more impressive, just about every one got promoted quickly. (As you'll discover, this is more legally sound than using traditional job descriptions.)

---

2 NY Times: Google's Quest to Build a Better Boss (http://budurl.com/agoxygen)

Rethinking the Hiring Problem

Since my early background was in engineering and manufacturing, the idea of converting raw material into something useful was always about yield. The less scrap and waste the better. The same is true in recruiting. Too many recruiters and the companies they work for think of hiring top talent as a numbers game with the objective of getting as many people to apply as possible so there will be a better chance of finding a good person. These concepts always seemed foreign to me. I always wanted to target as few great people as possible and make sure one of them gets hired. This was always more efficient, and with quality as the primary driver you always wound up with a great person hired in the shortest time possible, at some fair cost. Somehow this simple and straightforward concept got lost in the search for the next sourcing silver bullet or the beat of the big brass employer brand. I attribute much of this misguided thinking to some core misconceptions that have embedded themselves into the company culture:

1) **Breaking down the steps in the hiring process into independent silos rather than considering the process as a fully integrated business system.** This is akin to the concept of doing things serially rather than doing them in parallel. There is too much friction and loss between the silos.

2) **Companies relying on a talent surplus strategy to find people in a talent scarcity situation.** A surplus model is based on attracting the many and weeding out the weak to fill a specific role. A scarcity model is based on only attracting the best and tweaking the position to better fit their needs.

3) **An overreliance on indirect methods to find, assess, and hire top talent when direct methods are possible.** To quickly get your arms around this point, consider that job descriptions actually define people, competency models are based on probabilities, behavioral interviewing ignores the actual job and the manager, top candidates are not looking for lateral transfers, and first impressions don't predict performance.

4) **Lack of ownership on the part of the hiring manager.** Earlier this year I met the president of a fast-growing Russian-based technology company. In perfect English he asked me a very unusual question. It went something like this: "I read your book, *Hire With Your Head*, and if hiring top talent is so important, shouldn't every hiring manager be judged on how well they do it?" The answer, of course, is yes, and if hiring managers are not measured on this score at your company, hiring top talent is not number one.

Finding top people with tools like LinkedIn, Google+, and Career-Builder's Talent Network is actually not all that difficult. Unfortunately, changing strategies, thinking systematically, focusing on the real job, and requiring managers to take full responsibility for everyone they hire, needs to be the starting point.

The objective of this book is to provide a simple framework to jump-start this effort. It starts by rethinking strategies, processes, and responsibilities.

Performance-based Hiring Overview

At 20,000 feet hiring looks a lot different than looking at an open requisition or a candidate's resume to see if there's a match. Back in the early days, and after completing about 50-60 search projects, some obvious patterns began to emerge. These eventually became the foundation of the Performance-based Hiring process described in *Hire With Your Head*. Here's what stood out:

1) Hiring managers who consistently hired good people understood the real job requirements. As a result they did not rely on traditional job descriptions to screen or select candidates. They focused instead on what the person actually accomplished in comparison to what needed to be done. This is still true today.

2) The best candidates, whether employed or not, always considered the long-term career opportunity more important than the short-term package. None ever got excited by reading a traditional job description. This is still true today.

3) Very few managers were good interviewers, yet they all thought they were. This is still true today. At the time I wasn't very good either, but I needed to be, so I started benchmarking what the managers who hired good people did. They all seemed to ask variations of two basic questions, which I started using. As a result I then became a very good interviewer. These two questions now form the core of the performance-based interviewing process described in this book. Using these same two questions, all managers can quickly become great at assessing everything they need to know to make an accurate hiring decision.

4) There was very little logic or science involved in going from what was learned in the interview to making a yes-or-no hiring decision. Most companies used some type of informal debriefing process that involved some casual discussion. In reality this was nothing more than adding up a bunch of yes/no votes with "no" votes given more weight than "yes" votes, and those with more authority having more influence on the final result.

5) More hiring mistakes were made in the first 30 minutes of an interview than any other time, largely due to the impact of the candidate's first impression on the interviewer. Based on their initial reaction to a candidate, interviewers then followed a specific script, going out of their way to prove the candidate was incompetent if they didn't like the person, and seeking only positive information if they did.

6) Each step in the hiring process was largely independent from the other steps, adding inefficiency, time, and cost to the process. Advertising was hard to find and uninteresting. Compensation was the primary filter, not ability. Weeding out the weak was more important than attracting the best. Recruiters and hiring

managers didn't know what the other was looking for or looking at. As a result, the person ultimately hired was the best person who applied, not the best person available. This is still true today.

The Facts Don't Lie

The four-step Performance-based Hiring process as described throughout this book is a fully integrated business process and the facts speak for themselves:

- The fact that it's a system is one reason why it works.

- The fact that it's designed based on the needs of a top-performing person who's not looking is another reason that it works.

- The fact that the emphasis is on maximizing career growth, not compensation, is another reason why it works.

- But most important of all, the reason it works is that the foundation of the process is based on real job needs, not a job description. (Note: As far as I'm concerned, the over-reliance on job descriptions instead of commonsense is the primary reason companies can't hire enough good people, including military vets and diverse candidates.) However, to make it work seamlessly, the recruiter and hiring manager need to form a partnership based on trust, with both knowing they have an equal stake in the process and the outcome.

Maximizing Quality of Hire & Raising the Talent Bar

Individually, recruiters or hiring managers can't improve Quality of Hire very much no matter how capable they are. Together, they can do far better than working alone, but this is only one search at a time. Realistically, it seems foolhardy to delegate a company's talent acquisition strategy to each hiring manager and recruiter team who use their own individual techniques, and then hope for an optimum in-the-best-interests-of-the-company decision. Functional VPs and department heads certainly impose hiring guidelines that will improve the quality of each hiring decision made within their group. This is a good start, and much of what's presented in this book will help them get there or improve what they're already doing. In fact, much of what's presented in this book will allow any recruiter or any hiring manager do a better job filling one requisition at a time.

However, to make the process work companywide, a different talent acquisition strategy is required that underlies and drives each step in the process. Implementing an integrated system like Performance-based Hiring is a key part of this, since each step complements each other step, rather than compromising them. In this book I suggest the implementation of a talent scarcity hiring model as the core strategy. This is based on the assumption that the demand for top talent is far greater than the supply. In this situation, a company must offer career opportunities rather than lateral transfers; be open to flex the job somewhat to attract and hire more high achievers who might be light on experience and skills but high on potential; use an evidence-based interviewing and assessment process rather than generic behavioral interviewing; and make each hiring manager fully responsible for the people they hire.

Collectively, this is how you implement a Raising the Talent Bar strategy. In this approach, not only must candidates balance long-term opportunities with short-term rewards, but companies and hiring managers must do likewise. If hiring top talent is number one, hiring managers must be measured on how well they do it, and be trained to do it right. Without some intervention, most managers will emphasize their short-term business requirements and naturally overvalue experience for potential. They'll also be less prepared, give short shrift to the entire hiring process, and make emotional instead of logical decisions. This is one sure way to maintain the status-quo talent level. No amount of training will help with this as a starting mindset. But when combined with appropriate tracking metrics, a Scarcity of Talent strategy plus a business process like Performance-based Hiring, minimal training will result in far better hires and fewer mistakes companywide.

CANDIDATE ADVICE
How to Take Full Advantage of This Book

This is an odd book. Not only does it describe what you need to do to find and hire a person, it also describes what you need to do if you're the person being found and hired. Here's some big advisory points as you consider hiring from the candidate's side of the desk: 1) be prepared whether you're looking or not, and 2) don't be too hungry if you're looking, and don't be too hard to approach if you're not. Perceptions have a lot to do with who gets hired, so striking the right balance of open-mindedness, long-term career focus, and selectivity is important.

Throughout this book suggestions are provided to the candidate on how to handle a specific technique, whether it's answering a question or negotiating an offer. In some way these are countermeasures to use when the interviewer isn't using the techniques described in the book. In this case, the idea is to ask appropriate questions to get the interviewer or recruiter to use the proper techniques. This will help improve your odds of getting a job you deserve. Note: you will be judged fairly and accurately when the interviewer(s) are using the techniques described in this book, as long as you're prepared, open-minded, and appropriately interested.

Let me be perfectly clear on the purpose of this book regarding all of the candidate-facing advice: it is not intended to help you get a job you don't deserve or are not qualified for. It only will help you get a job you deserve. This by itself is a tall order, which is why I, as a recruiter, never present an unqualified candidate to a hiring manager. Unfortunately, too many candidates who are perfectly qualified have fallen far short of the presentation skills necessary to land the opportunity presented to them. This book is specifically written to them, to all of the hiring managers who will be hiring them, and to all of the recruiters who will help them make the right career choice.

....

Key Summary Points

- You can't use a talent surplus approach for hiring top people in a talent scarcity situation. When the demand for talent is greater than the supply you must consider the hiring process from the perspective of a top person who has multiple opportunities. The big point: offer careers, not just another job. Too many companies default to the surplus model for hiring, offering lateral transfers and weeding out the weak. In the process, the best never apply.

- While much has changed over the years, much hasn't. Top people are still very discriminating when it comes to changing jobs. Top people still don't look for work the way average people look for work. And top people are still not willing to apply for a position before they learn about the potential upside first. However, how you find these people and reach them has changed profoundly. Merging the new with the old is how you not only find them, but hire them, too.

- A large majority of HR and recruiting leaders believe that their hiring problems will be solved by some magical new sourcing tool or the latest social media approach. They'll be disappointed. Their quest for the next sourcing silver bullet will be as disappointing as the last one. Hiring top talent needs to be a comprehensive business system integrating all facets of the process from finding and sourcing candidates, including screening and selection, and recruiting and closing. Performance-based Hiring is a process that addresses all of these needs.

- Walk the talk. There's more to hiring top talent and raising a company's talent bar than a mission statement and a competency model. Executives need to rethink their company's hiring programs and processes from top to bottom, inside-out, and backwards. Part of this is metrics, part of it is management, but the most important part is converting talk into action.

- Hiring managers need to take the responsibility for hiring outstanding people. This should be a core component of their performance review. While some hiring managers will do this on their own because they know hiring the best is not just idle talk, many won't, and many aren't capable of hiring people stronger than they are. On top of this, short-term pressures to deliver often outweigh the need to upgrade the talent level. External measurement systems need to be established to ensure a company's talent acquisition strategy is implemented and executed properly.

- If you're a candidate, recognize that most companies don't do it right. So if you don't get the job you deserve or the chance to get interviewed, it's because you expected the process to work properly. It doesn't, so play the hiring game to win. This starts by knowing how the game is played and knowing all of the rules, both written and unwritten, and then breaking them.

Chapter 1

Introduction to Performance-based Hiring

Whether you're a manager interviewing candidates, a recruiter trying to find these candidates, a member of the interviewing team, or a person looking for a job, you need to be great at interviewing. Hiring the wrong person due to an incorrect assessment, or not getting a job due to poor interviewing skills, is a waste of everyone's time and effort, worsened by the lost opportunity the bad decision represents. In this book you'll find out exactly what you need to do to ace the interview, whichever side of the desk you're on.

If you're interviewing a candidate, you need to quickly and accurately assess competency. The relatively obvious reason for this, though, is not the most important reason. The obvious reason is to ensure that the candidate is competent to do the work, motivated to do the work, and can work well within the culture and style of the organization. The less obvious reason is twofold:

- First, to ensure that those with a yes/no vote base it on evidence, not emotions.

- Second, to demonstrate to the person being interviewed that the position you're trying to fill represents a worthy career move. So worthy, in fact, that money is not the primary reason for accepting or rejecting an offer, if one is extended.

Hiring managers should not need their recruiters or other members of the hiring team to prevent them from making easily preventable hiring blunders, but unfortunately they do. Most overvalue their intuition, the rest overvalue the candidate's technical competency, and just about everyone overvalues presentation over performance. Recruiters and everyone else on the hiring team are not exempt from these problems. Since little of this overvaluing gets at fit—either with the job, the company's approach to doing business, or the relationship between the new hire and the hiring manager—subsequent on-the-job performance is unpredictable. Typically, the result is hiring people who are only partially competent, or people who are competent, but not as motivated as necessary to achieve exceptional performance due to lack of fit in some way.

CANDIDATE ADVICE
Take Responsibility for Bad Interviewers

The person being interviewed is not spared from the consequences of these bad decisions, nor the responsibility for making a proper presentation. As a candidate you need to make sure you present yourself in the proper light, making sure the interviewing team has all of the information necessary to make a well-reasoned decision about you. As part of this, you need to gather the information necessary to judge the opportunity properly, from both a short- and long-term perspective. Of course your personal circumstances will dictate much of this decision-making, but taking a job out of desperation—or the one offering the most money—should be at the bottom of the list.

....

On the face of it, this cacophony of needs, combined with the lack of complete information and the means to obtain it, makes an accurate hiring decision problematic at best. As a result, everyone looks for shortcuts. In doing so, they hire the wrong people, overlook better candidates, or never even meet other stronger candidates who opt out very early in the process because they didn't initially see the opportunity presented as a worthy career move.

Whether you're the candidate or an interviewer, Performance-based Hiring offers a fundamentally different way to address and overcome every one of these complex and important issues. I'll use the first part of this book to focus on providing insight to those doing the interviewing, followed up with advice to the candidate on how to navigate the tricky waters of human nature and ill-advised decision-making.

What is Performance-based Hiring and Is It the Solution?

In my book, *Hire With Your Head*, I describe the Performance-based Hiring process completely, from first contact to the final close and through the onboarding process. I developed Performance-based Hiring over a 20-year stint as an executive recruiter from 1978-1998. It was used by everyone in my search firm on over 1,500 placements. Approximately half of these were contingent, and the balance retained search assignments. Less than five percent of the 1,500 got terminated for poor performance during the first year. In most of these cases, weak performance was rarely due to lack of technical competency. Instead, it was a poor fit with the hiring manager where their individual styles clashed. Working with the team and lack of motivation to do the work required represented the balance of the problems. The Performance-based Hiring process described in this book has been further developed to address these common and critical issues.

Performance-based Hiring is now used today around the world by companies and third-party recruiting firms. In the past 10 years we've trained over 10,000 hiring managers and 2,500 recruiters. We're now training hiring managers and recruiters in India, Russia, China, and throughout Europe, South America, and North America. Interestingly, everyone seems to have the same hiring problems: not enough good people, nor the best means to find and assess them. Performance-based Hiring offers a reasonable and cost-effective solution. There are probably other ways to accomplish the same task but in the last 30 years nothing better has emerged, other than when the supply of great talent exceeds the demand. In that case, it doesn't really matter what you do, you'll wind up making a pretty good decision, even if it's not the best one.

Let me be perfectly clear. Better competency models, more behavioral interview training, additional assessments, and more focus on technical skills will not solve these problems. Yet many company leaders still believe they will. The problem is too many HR leaders put the tactics before the strategy. If you want to hire stronger people and raise a company's talent level, this needs to be the strategy and the focus. This means going on the offense rather than playing defense.

During my 20 years as a full-time recruiter and recruiting manager, we rarely had to present more than 3-4 candidates for any search. As part of our continuous improvement program, we also studied every aspect of the hiring process, not only to optimize it, but to ensure that everyone was making a proper and appropriate business decision. On the company side, this had to do with making an accurate, unbiased assessment and selecting the best person possible for the position. For the candidate, it involved ensuring that the person being hired balanced the short- and long-term aspects of the job properly and that the job itself represented the best career move among competing opportunities. Mistakes were made when compensation became the dominant decision factor combined with superficial knowledge about real job needs and what it took to be successful. Few mistakes were made, either by the company or the candidate, when the focus of the decision emphasized the career opportunity and the impact the person could make, not the compensation. Bottom line, this is what Performance-based Hiring is all about.

Candidate Advice

> Before you ever accept another job, ask yourself this question: "Forget the money. Is this a job I want?" If not, you'll be disappointed no matter how much you get paid.

Rather than rehash *Hire With Your Head*, here's the process in a nutshell:

First, you must banish traditional job descriptions listing skills, duties, and responsibilities from the adverting, assessment, and selection process. These need to be replaced with performance profiles describing on-the-job success. A performance profile typically consists of 5-6 performance objectives such as, "Launch the new Apple iPad series of applications by year end." This is much better than saying, "Must have 5 years of product marketing background in the digital ecommerce space, a technical undergraduate degree, and an MBA." Tools are provided in the chapter on preparing performance profiles, but the big idea is that skills, duties, and responsibilities are distractors and poorly designed disqualifiers. They preclude the best from applying, and having them doesn't predict performance. Performance profiles, on the other hand, open up the candidate pool to everyone who has achieved comparable performance.

Second, you only need to conduct a thorough work-history review and use two basic questions to assess competency and motivation for all the performance objectives listed in the performance profile. Note: you need to ask the questions multiple times to cover all of the performance objectives. While the questions are simple, getting the answers is sometimes a challenge since you need to "train" candidates to give you the correct information.

Third, evidence gathered from the work-history review and the two questions is used to measure Quality of Hire and determine who should be hired. The foundation of the assessment is a review of core competencies and situational fit factors that have been shown to accurately predict on-the-job performance. This differs substantially from traditional competency models and behavioral interviewing approaches since these don't effectively link the candidate's answers to actual job requirements. The assessment is further optimized by organizing the interview among the different interviewers to ensure all of the appropriate information is collected properly. This precludes the faulty approach of adding up yes/no votes from each interviewer, especially when many of these votes are superficial, biased, tainted, or emotionally-based.

Fourth, good candidates always have multiple offers and typically want more money than available, at least initially. However, if the job represents a significant career move, the money issue becomes less important in the overall decision-making process. This necessitates the importance of using the interview to not only assess the candidate, but also to start the recruiting process. Every serious candidate needs to see the job as much more than a lateral transfer. Too often the recruiting activity is left until the end of the assessment process, and then only for the last candidate remaining. This is a great way to have the best candidates opt out too soon, and pay an unnecessary compensation premium to the last person remaining and ultimately hired. Frequently the underlying recruiting problem is based on arrogance, the assumption that everyone wants to work at the company and they are willing to accept lateral transfers, even the high achievers.

Performance-based Hiring is a business process for hiring top talent. It's based on the assumption that the demand for talent is far greater than the supply. As a result the focus of every step is on attracting, assessing, and hiring top people who have multiple opportunities.

Don't Put the Cart Before the Horse

Here's a story that gives horses a bad name. From what I've seen, the root cause of most hiring problems starts by using the wrong talent strategy. Most companies use a Surplus of Talent strategy in a Scarcity of Talent world. I call this the Staffing Spiral of Doom Catch-22. (I put together a video with LinkedIn that summarizing this idea.) (http://budurl.com/LICatch22)

The underlying assumption behind a surplus model is to get as many people to apply as possible and weed out the weakest, with the hope that a few good ones will remain. This doesn't work, of course, if the surplus assumption is wrong. If your company posts boring job descriptions, hiring managers are disengaged, and candidates are forced to apply and then screened out on factors that don't predict success, you're using a surplus model. This will work if there are plenty of good people to choose from, but if not, you're just spinning your wheels, mistaking activity for progress.

A talent scarcity strategy starts with the premise that the demand for top talent is greater than the supply. As a result, the company needs to put the necessary resources and processes in place to attract and hire these people despite the competition. Since the best people always have multiple opportunities, they are not the least bit interested in jumping through hoops for something that appears to be a lateral transfer. Yet most companies, even in the face of a talent shortage problem, continue to use traditional skills-based job descriptions for advertising, screening, and selection purposes. This is certainly putting the cart before the horse, with the driver (aka, the recruiter) somewhere behind both, doing what's necessary to clean up the mess. As you'll see even from a compliance standpoint (OFCCP and EEOC), putting the horse in front increases not only compliance, but your company's share of top talent.

The graphic below summarizes the hiring decision-making process into four time-phased areas along with three major decision points. There are also three primary decision-makers involved throughout this process: the hiring manager, the recruiter, and the candidate. All three continually make bad horse-and-cart decisions, compounding the complexity of the problem.

The problem with a Surplus of Talent strategy is the focus on "Before Day 1" criteria to screen out people when the best people are using "Year 1 and Beyond" criteria before they'll screen themselves in, and accept an offer. It doesn't take much to figure out that this backwards thinking eliminates just about everyone who is any good. This is the Catch-22 problem mentioned above, screening out good people for skills most of them don't have. And even if they do have them, they're more interested in how they'll be leveraging these skills, not just doing more of the same. Even worse, this approach eliminates high-potential candidates who are light on experience, but who have tremendous upside. Most managers are willing to see these candidates, and are even willing to modify the job a bit to get them hired. Unfortunately, using skills-based advertising and screening blocks these people from consideration. Add diversity candidates and returning military vets to the group of people equally blocked.

This is a huge problem that companies go out of their way to solve reactively even though a proactive solution is obvious and relatively simple: stop using job descriptions listing skills and experience factors for advertising and screening purposes.

A 20,000 Foot View of the Hiring Process from Beginning to End

Understanding the graphic will help clarify the horse-cart-driver positioning problem and offer some obvious solutions. Everyone involved in hiring is in a continuous state of making quick decisions at every step in the process. Unfortunately, very few are using the same information or the correct information at the right time. As a result many good people are excluded too soon either by their own or someone else's choice. The big point: most people are using Before Day 1 and Day 1 criteria when they all should be using Year 1 and Beyond. This equates to the classic business problem of making long-term, strategic decisions using short-term, tactical information. For a company, this is a sure-fire way to neither see nor hire the best person possible. For the candidate, it's missing out on a great career opportunity that superficially seems like a lateral transfer.

TIME-PHASED HIRING AND DECISION-MAKING PROCESS

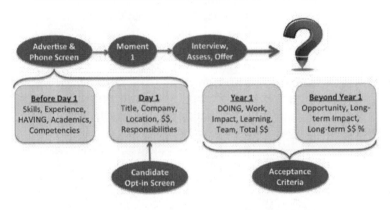

Think Backwards – Emphasize Year 1 and Beyond

Here are how these big four time-based decision buckets are misused:

Before Day 1: This is what the candidate needs to have in terms of skills and experience before being allowed to enter the assessment process. It also represents the bulk of what's described in the posted job description and what's used to screen out the undesirables. From a compliance standpoint this is considered "objective" even though it's likely not valid. (See the general legal validation by David Goldstein of Littler Mendelson of Performance-based Hiring in the Appendix for more on this topic.) If you've ever hired or promoted a person into a role who's been successful with less than or different skills than what's listed, you know that the requirements listed in typical job descriptions are largely guesswork, often without any scientific basis. Just imagine how many good people get screened out using these "flawed" objective criteria.

On the flip side, consider how many high-potential people screened themselves out because the job appeared to be a lateral transfer when they read the public job posting.

Day 1: This is what the person hired gets on the first day on the job: a salary, in some office, at some company, in some city, with some generic title. Most good candidates want to know this information right away to see if it's worth spending more time discussing it with a recruiter. What's surprising is that while this criteria is used as an initial filter for candidates, it's second or third, or unimportant, when the person actually decides whether to take the job, especially if there are other competing opportunities available. So unless the recruiter can bridge this "engage vs. accept" logic gap, you'll lose another chunk of great people.

Year 1: This is what the person actually does on the job and with whom they do it. This is the work itself, including what the person is going to learn and do. The hiring manager and the team are a critical part of this. Collectively, this is what drives satisfaction, and if the work is important, exciting, and done well, it leads to long-term growth. Equally important, it's the primary information a top person uses to compare different opportunities, including a counteroffer, if extended. Surprisingly, most companies don't even discuss this stuff in much detail with anyone other than with final candidates. By then, many of the best people have opted out on their own, or never entered the fray in the first place.

Here's the dilemma. Recruiters need to persist when speaking with candidates for the first time, to make sure they don't opt out without knowing this Year 1 information. Unfortunately, hiring managers don't tell their recruiters this information, assuming they already know it. Even if they don't, the managers believe the recruiters wouldn't know what to do with it anyway. Candidates and prospects need to understand some of this information before deciding to get serious about an opportunity. But even if they ask the recruiter to tell them some real details about the job, most of the time all they get back is generic boilerplate. This is certainly not enough information to overcome their concerns, especially if they're not actively looking for another job. In my mind, recruiters have to take the lead here and force the hiring manager to provide the information and then force the candidate to listen before deciding. This is what I refer to as controlling the conversation.

You Need to Pull Some Strings to Ensure the Right Decision is Made

Beyond Year 1: This is what the person can become if he/she successfully completes the challenges of Year 1. This represents the future possibilities and is a large part of the Employee Value Proposition (EVP), describing what's in it for the candidate if successful in Year 1. The EVP is the career growth opportunity collectively represented by the job, the hiring manager, the team, and the company. While implied in many postings and discussed superficially during the interview, it's mostly vague and generic, and as a result, downplayed by the recruiter, the hiring manager, and the candidate. This is a lost opportunity. If you want to attract the attention of more of the best people at the early stages of your hiring process, the EVP should be trumpeted in your postings, emails, talent hubs, career pages, and voice mails. Unfortunately, this is typically not the case. More often, whatever is posted is more PR and company propaganda that is too generic and bland to appeal to top people who always have multiple opportunities. The real good stuff is typically hidden somewhere behind closed doors, only revealed when and if needed to close a person. The common excuse for not doing this is that it sounds like a promise, rather than a potential opportunity, and could get the company in trouble if the person doesn't reap some of the rewards promised. The simple solution: tell candidates that the potential for rapid growth exists for those that achieve stellar performance in Year 1.

CANDIDATE ADVICE
Ask the Right Questions When Contacted by a Recruiter

Even if the recruiter doesn't persist, candidates and semi-interested passive prospects should also fight the natural tendency to screen out opportunities based on Day 1 criteria. The best people always consider the long-term opportunity more important than the short-term factors when deciding to accept an offer or not. This is a good decision-making practice for everyone to follow. If you're a candidate, you'll gain in at least four important ways by asking about Year 1 and Beyond before you ask about Day 1, to determine your initial interest in a new job opportunity. First, it won't seem like you're desperate, which is important from a negotiating stand-point. Second, you'll seem like a logical, career-oriented person, which is an important signal to send to the recruiter. Third, and most important, it actually might be a great job. And fourth, if it's not a great job, you'll be able to build out your network. You never know what else might be available in the future.

Avoiding the Classic "Tell Me About Day 1" Recruiting Conundrum

Now let's bring some order to this mishmash of illogical and competing information and take it into the real world of hiring. To start, let's ignore for now what happens when some recruiter reviews a resume or LinkedIn profile and decides whether or not to call someone. After this troublesome step, the big three decision points in the hiring process include the initial phone contact and preliminary job discussion, the full interview and the assessment and selection process, and the final offer and negotiating process.

As you'll see, ego and power immediately get in the way, preventing everyone from making the optimum decision. That's why it is so important to leave your ego in the parking lot. Everyone needs to consider everyone else as equals and equally important. The problem is that at different phases in the hiring process there is a different starring role, and there is an ebb and flow to this that the players often lose sight of as everyone fights to stay in the limelight:

- Recruiters naturally think they own the front end

- Hiring managers think they own everything

- Candidates, especially those who are fully employed and with multiple options, clearly think they're in charge

Acting as the director in this unfolding scene, I'll give the true starring role to the hot prospect, but I'll make sure I don't tell the person this until the movie is over. Until then, everyone needs to be treated as equals, or co-stars, so to speak. I'll hand over the actual on-scene director's role to the recruiter shortly, but for now let's make sure everyone gets equal billing in the first scene.

Here's why this "co-star" idea is so important. In a talent-scarcity world, the top person makes most of the critical early decisions. Unfortunately more times than not, they make the wrong ones, using Day 1 decision-making data when they should be using Year 1 and Beyond. If the recruiter and hiring manager don't recognize the importance of these distinctions, they'll never develop the information ahead of time to address the candidate's questions adequately. On the other hand, if the hot prospect quickly decides whether to go forward based on Before

Day 1 and Day 1 criteria, the person is making a critical long-term decision using short-term information.

If the prospect appears strong on paper and uninterested in the Day 1 offerings, the recruiter or hiring manager succumb to the bait and attempt to oversell the person on the merits of the opportunity, describing the compensation package and other nifty incentives. This is a knee-jerk reaction that can be avoided by starting every discussion on the basis that it's only exploratory. Then state that a mutual agreement will be made to move forward based on the career merits of the job opening. Too many recruiters have a different mindset, short-circuiting this approach. Their objective is to fill an open position as quickly as possible.

Whether you're a candidate, prospect, or recruiter, slowing down at this point of initial contact is important. Haste leads to over-selling and close-mindedness. This is at the root of why companies can't get enough top people initially interested in what's being offered. Considering each other as equal co-stars, each with different interests, helps all parties to obtain the right information to mutually decide if it makes sense to proceed to the next step. This typically requires the hiring manager to get involved earlier than normal, agreeing to engage in "exploratory" discussions with anyone the recruiter recommends. Of course, the recruiter has an obligation to only present strong candidates under this situation. This is typically very hard for hiring managers to accept as a condition, since they're the ones deciding to hire someone or not and believe they have all of the power. On top of this, many make the arrogant assumption that there are plenty of good people chomping at the bit to work for the company and in the role described for the compensation offered. That's why they're reluctant to give the recruiter anything other than Before Day 1 and Day 1 criteria to screen candidates out. Under these common circumstances recruiters feel subordinate to the hiring manager, and without authority or other options, all they can do is screen out candidates who don't have the Before Day 1 skills.

Consider what's lost using this "traditional" approach:

- Top people who have all of the skills, but who aren't interested in what appears to be a lateral transfer.

- Top people who have a different mix of skills, including diversity candidates and military vets, who could be extremely successful if Year 1 and Beyond criteria was used to screen them in rather than weeding them out using Day 1 and Before Day 1 criteria.

- High-potential people who are a little light in the skills and experience department who require some extra coaching or training. While the job might need to be flexed to accommodate them, this group represents the future of the company.

Hiring managers need to recognize that finding and hiring a top person takes teamwork, especially partnering with a recruiter. Also important for hiring managers to understand is that the best people, whether they're active or passive, aren't looking for lateral transfers unless there's significantly more near-term upside associated with it. That's why defining Year 1 and Beyond before starting a search is so important.

CANDIDATE ADVICE
Be Open-minded

As part of this, prospects also need to recognize that if the job represents a significant career move, compensation will be third or fourth on their acceptance criteria list, so don't make it, or the location, the first thing discussed when first contacted by someone from the company. If you are contacted by a recruiter, ask about the job, the challenges, why the job is open, and how the job relates to an important company project or the company's mission. Use this as the reason to move forward or not. Continue the conversation even if the job doesn't sound perfect but the company is doing some interesting things. Frequently the job can be modified to better suit a strong person's interests and abilities, or there might be something else available.

....

While the decision-making power shifts at each step in the process, understanding and respecting everyone's role and viewpoint is a critical first step in untangling the cart-horse-driver problem we've self-created.

Let's get started.

Shifting Everyone's Emphasis to Year 1 and Beyond

Here's the dilemma exposed by the hiring process flow chart: there's too much emphasis on what the person brings to the table and what the person hired obtains on Day 1. The Catch-22 problem is that there are great numbers of people who can do the work required (Year 1) who don't have the exact skills listed on the job description (Before Day 1). Many of these people, especially the best ones, would be interested in considering the opportunity represented by Year 1 and Beyond, but never get the chance. For one thing, jobs aren't advertised this way. For another, some recruiter or hiring manager screened them out based on the wrong factors. Worse, the best prospects screened themselves out, since the offering as described represented a lateral transfer.

E mphasizing Before Day 1 requirements, screening out on Day 1 criteria, and hoping the best prospects will somehow emerge and figure out the Year 1 and Beyond opportunity on their own severely limits the pool of people being considered.

Yet this represents the fundamental hiring process used by most companies. This problem is aggravated when these same companies use these same processes to hire passive candidates, who aren't looking for another job, but might be open to evaluate a job if it represents a true Year 1 and Beyond career opportunity.

The key from a compliance standpoint is to ensure objective criteria is used to screen people out or in. However, objective criteria is not limited to skills, experiences, and academics. Year 1 criteria listing key tasks and measurable performance objectives are equally as objective. In fact, one could easily argue that "installing an SAP consolidations module in six months" is more objective than "must have a CPA and five years ERP systems background." More important, the "Year 1" project is far more exciting from the candidate's perspective than meeting the "Before Day 1" experience standard. (Note: the General Legal Validation by David Goldstein of Littler Mendelson not only supports this viewpoint, but contends it's far more objective and more defensible.)

By defining Year 1 and Beyond before defining Day 1 and Before, the horse is put in its proper place, and there's no mess left behind. And when the Year 1 and Beyond criteria is used for advertising and screening, the pool of exceptional prospects increases dramatically. For one thing, it opens up the door to more minority, military, and diversity candidates who have a different mix of leadership experiences but are fully qualified to handle the challenges defined with minimal training. As far as mixing metaphors goes, not only is the horse put in its proper position this way, but you can then have and eat your cake, plus all of the icing.

Managing the Moment – Controlling Interviewer Bias

More hiring mistakes are made in the first 30 minutes of the face-to-face interview than at any other time. This is what I refer to as "Moment 1" mistakes. Most of them are caused by overvaluing first impressions.

Most interviewers unconsciously react to the candidate's first impression, good and bad. If bad, they become uptight, convinced the person is not qualified. This unconscious bias causes them to ask tougher questions, going out of their way to prove the candidate is not qualified. They minimize the positives and maximize the negatives. Sometime during the interview this bias dissipates, but for those candidates that start out in the doghouse it's often too late, with the person never being seriously considered or evaluated.

In comparison, prospects who are prepared, confident, friendly, outgoing, communicative, and professional in appearance tend to be instantly considered viable candidates for the open position, even if they lack basic skills. Under the influence of a positive first impression, interviewers relax, become more open-minded, and tend to ask easier questions, maximizing the positives and minimizing the negatives. Their unconscious objective is to prove the candidate is qualified. For those given the initial free ride, their deficiencies are frequently uncovered if the company has a multi-step and rigorous selection process, but not always. If you've ever hired someone who makes a great presentation during the interview, but doesn't deliver the results needed, you've experienced the negative impact of this first impression bias first-hand. Even if you haven't been caught red-handed holding the bag here, think about all of the great people you didn't hire only because they were human, getting a little nervous at the beginning of the interview or because they didn't fit someone's stereotype of the perfect candidate.

Of course, many of you reading about this concept for the first time won't agree with me about the minimal importance of first impressions. You'll loudly protest that good first impressions are essential for anyone in a sales position, working with executives, or being part of multi-functional teams. Even though you're mistaken, and will not be able to find any research or evidence that your flawed belief is correct, you'll provide plenty of anecdotal evidence to justify your position. For you naysayers, I'll ask you to just delay your decision about the candidate until the end of the interview. By then you won't be affected, seduced, or biased by the candidate's first impression.

What you'll discover after this delay is that about one-third of the people you interview aren't nearly as great as you initially thought. Another one-third will be a lot better than you first imagined, and you might even want to hire a few of them. The remaining one-third will turn out to be pretty much as you first imagined, but don't take any credit for this instant insight; assign it to statistics and probability instead.

I'm not trying to suggest that working with clients, executives, and different types of people is unimportant. All I'm suggesting is that you can't assess this objectively when you're being affected by what you're trying to measure. Rather than focus on the person's first impression, find out if the person has a track record of working with great clients, or has worked with top executives, or has been assigned to a variety of critical multi-functional teams, or ideally, can meet the performance objectives required for success. If they have, you'll discover the person's first impression is exactly what it needs to be, even if it doesn't meet your standards. Then start questioning how you came up with the standards you're using to begin with. By measuring how the person's first impression helped or hindered their job performance, rather than if it's strong or weak in your mind, you'll find out that your definition of a good first impression might either be biased, illegal, or inappropriate. Don't eliminate good people for superficial reasons. It's important to give everyone a fair and objective evaluation, regardless of their age, race, accent, or physical characteristics. What should be measured is their ability to meet the performance objectives defined by Year 1, not how they present themselves during the interview.

Minimizing Moment 1 Mistakes

Regardless of how appropriate and necessary, putting first impressions in the parking lot is not easy to do. In addition to the caveat "wait until the end of the interview to measure first impressions," here are a few other techniques you can use to minimize the problems associated with making "Moment 1" mistakes:

1) **Wait 30 minutes.** Put a little yellow sticky on every candidate's resume to remind you to delay any rush to judgment for at least 30 minutes. During the initial 30 minutes of the interview conduct a work-history review looking for the Achiever Pattern, and ask one job-related Most Significant Accomplishment question. Your emotional reaction to the candidate will have changed completely by then. (This technique will make a lot more sense after you've read the next few chapters.)

2) **Use the "plus or minus" mind reversal technique.** When you first meet a candidate note your initial reaction to the person with some type of plus or minus indictor. Then force yourself to do the exact opposite of what you'd normally do. For people you don't like, ask them easier questions, going out of your way to prove they're fully competent. Ask those you do like tougher questions, going out of your way to prove they're not the least bit qualified for the job. This mental reversal is how you offset your natural reactions to first impressions. You'll then be able to ask everyone the same objective questions.

3) **Treat candidates as consultants.** Assume everyone you're meeting is an expert for the job at hand. This is the way you treat someone who would be consulting for you doing similar work. Under the consultant umbrella you assume competence, you give respect, and you listen attentively, assuming the person has more expertise than you do. Consultants need to screw up pretty badly to be discredited, so give everyone the benefit of the doubt initially. You also don't require that a consultant be a close co-worker, so first impressions and friendliness are of less importance in your ultimate decision. By the end of the first interview, you'll objectively know if the candidate will make the short list.

4) **Phone screen the candidate first.** You would never invite a person for an onsite interview if you didn't think they were reasonably qualified. Conducting a 30-40 minute phone screen helps you make this assessment. When you meet a person about whom you already know something, first impressions are naturally far

less impactful. Since you have some time already invested in the person, you naturally feel more obligated to conduct an objective assessment when you meet face to face. I have a personal rule to never meet a candidate in person until I've conducted an in-depth phone screen as a means to increase objectivity.

5) **Don't let the candidate get nervous.** Recognize that most of the people you want to hire are not professional interviewers and many will get somewhat nervous at the beginning of the interview. Expect it, and view this as a positive, not a negative. If it persists for too long, it is a problem, which is why holding off on even a preliminary judgment for at least 30 minutes is a good idea. (Professional interviewers should be the ones that get you nervous, since you're not sure whether you're hearing fact or fiction.) Rather than starting the interview right away, take the person on a tour, or to the cafeteria to get a cup of coffee. Go out of your way to ensure your candidate is comfortable and relaxed. This way you'll better understand what your candidate has actually accomplished without the filter of the first impression bias in your way.

CANDIDATE ADVICE
Managing Moment 1

For candidates being interviewed, here are some things you can do to overcome or prevent temporary nervousness. You should do all of these things anyway, whether or not you're prone to get somewhat nervous at the beginning of the interview. There's a full section on this topic in the chapter focusing on what a candidate needs to do to get ready for the performance-based interview, but the following will give you some quick ideas on what you need to do to minimize any problems associated with getting a bit nervous at the beginning of the interview.

Understand it. Temporary interview nervousness is usually due to the emotional reaction referred to as the "friend vs. foe" or "fight-or-flight" response. Meeting any stranger in an awkward situation, or entering unfamiliar territory, initially puts you on guard, more so in an interview where there's so much at stake. If the person turns out to be friendly, you relax and communicate normally. If the person challenges you, you become uptight, fearful, or somewhat nervous, not knowing what's coming next. This causes your pulse to speed up, your voice to tighten, your answers to shorten or become superficial, you lose your confidence, you become forgetful, and worst of all, perhaps start to sweat. All of this is telling your body to leave the room! None of these uncontrollable things are helpful for making that all important "good first impression." The same "on guard" reaction happens when you're dealing with any new situation, but the reaction is heightened when your ego is involved. Once you realize the threat isn't real you calm down, but in the case of an interview, it's sometimes too late. Being prepared and knowing what's going to happen can minimize the blow and allow you to fake it until your emotions are back to normal.

Practice and prepare. The chapter on prepping for the interview needs to be your bible, fully absorbed and owned. It describes a multi-step process including knowing your resume so well you don't need to look at it, providing detailed, specific examples of actual accomplishments demonstrating your strengths and how you manage your weaknesses, and knowing how to answer any question in a logical 1-2 minute format. Then you need to practice all of this so you can mix and match the information regardless of the questions asked. Getting a little bit nervous or anxious before an interview is very common, but this leads to a bit of forgetfulness. All of this practice and preparation will help you to recover your composure more quickly by increasing your confidence. No one else will be the wiser. Rick Gillis' book, *Job!: Learn How to Find Your Next Job in 1 Day*, also provides some valuable advice on how you can prepare for the interview.

Do your company homework. Become familiar with the company's business model, product lines, financial performance, and industry standing. Spending 1-2 hours getting ready for your first interview for an important job is the bare minimum. As a benchmark, consider how much time it takes to get ready to prepare for a company presentation on some important matter. Then realize a job interview is more important, so invest the time necessary to do it right. Review the career section in detail, reread the job description, and look at other openings to find out about hiring trends. Watch the employee videos to gain a sense of the culture. Try to find some connections with the job for which you're interviewing to a bigger project, the company strategy, or how it supports the company image or vision. For example, an entry-level customer care position is a critical job when it helps the company meet its objective of maximizing customer satisfaction. Knowing the company will increase your confidence, reduce the tendency to get nervous, and allow you to ask insightful questions.

Ask great questions. Asking any question puts the burden on the other person to respond. The 30 seconds it takes for someone to respond is sometimes all it takes to recover your thought process. At the beginning of the interview you can ask something like, "Would you mind telling me a little bit about the challenges in the job? The recruiter was a bit vague on this point." This will definitely give you time to collect your thoughts as the person responds. During the interview I suggest three types of questions. Opening questions are used to better understand the job by asking something relevant that is not found on the company website. These can be used to give you breathing room if necessary and/or to demonstrate you're a candidate who knows what you're looking for in a new job. Mid-interview questions are helpful to clarify any questions the interviewer asks that are job-specific. End-of-interview questions allow you to demonstrate your command of the situation, demonstrate your interest, and figure out if you'll be invited back.

Deal with it. Practice getting nervous. Put yourself in situations where you're likely to get nervous, like speaking to a group, practicing interviewing with your kids where they're asking the questions, or asking someone for a date. It doesn't matter what you do to get nervous as long as you understand that the nervousness is short-lived and you can manage it. Experiencing this has a calming effect when you know you can get through it. Sometimes it's all you need to recover in a few seconds.

Dress the Part. If your appearance is not ideal – which is just about everyone – you'll need to do everything described above, plus add more action items to your prep-for-the-interview checklist. Being clean and neat is part of this. Don't overdress or be too casual, either. You need to use your best judgment here, but asking what's appropriate business attire certainly can't hurt. If you feel your appearance is a real negative, you can minimize this by making sure you're interviewed on the phone first. This can't be a superficial interview, either. You must make sure that you've asked about the performance expectations for the job, and have described some of your most relevant accomplishments. This will ensure that the focus of the face-to-face interview will largely be about your ability to achieve comparable results, not your physical appearance. Don't avoid this, no matter how uncomfortable it is to discuss. Proactively minimizing the impact of the negative first impression bias is something every candidate needs to consider if you think you'll be judged this way. The goal of the phone interview from the candidate's perspective is to ensure you're invited onsite due to some of your relevant accomplishments.

....

Summary – Performance-based Hiring from All Sides

- If you want to improve your ability to hire stronger people, the collective conclusion is obvious: define the performance required for success, use this for recruitment advertising and screening, and then find people who have done something comparable. In the process you'll discover they have exactly the right level of skills, experience, and motivation to do the job. This is what Performance-based Hiring is all about.

- Hiring managers not only need to understand the job from a Year 1 and Beyond perspective, but they also need to control Moment 1. Most hiring errors occur in the first 30 minutes of the interview due to preconceptions based on first impressions. Waiting 30 minutes before making any judgment and asking every candidate detailed performance-based questions will eliminate many of these hiring mistakes.

- If you're a candidate you need to make sure you understand what level of performance is required for on-the-job success, and then prove you're both competent and motivated to do this work. Make sure you ask about the Year 1 criteria when first contacted by a recruiter. Don't worry about Day 1, the location of the job, or the company, either. These will only become important if the job offers a true career move, so find this out first. Even if the job at first glance isn't up your alley, you never know what can happen a week or two, or months, later. Following this last piece of advice might be how you get your next great job.

- Recruiters need to control the process from beginning to end by clarifying Year 1 and Beyond criteria before ever contacting a possible candidate. Then they have to make sure they screen these same candidates on this same criteria, and that the candidates themselves use the same Year 1 and Beyond criteria before they screen themselves out. This is why I consider the recruiter the director or orchestra leader in the process, making sure everyone makes the right decisions with the right information. It starts by making sure everyone who has a role in assessing the candidate is reasonably capable of doing it reasonably well.

Chapter 2

The General Formula
for Hiring Success

The original subtitle for the first edition (1997) of *Hire With Your Head* was "A Rational Way to Make a Gut Decision." The point of this was to suggest that there are ways to minimize the risk of hiring someone who isn't a "perfect" fit by substituting evidence of exceptional past performance and a pattern of achievement in a variety of comparable situations. The suggested means of getting there was through the use of a form of generic competency model in combination with factors that best predict actual fit with the job. While the model has been revised over the years, this concept is summarized in The General Formula for Hiring Success shown in the graphic below.

Over the past 30 years, I've reviewed dozens of competency models. While all were well-intended, most were vague, consisting of ill-defined and overlapping factors driven more by hope and expectations rather than evidence or practicality. A few were expertly developed, but difficult to use when assessing candidates since they were too generic. Making matters worse, in most cases, interviewers were given very little direction on how to make the assessment, with the majority of interviewers using their own definitions and assessment techniques.

The Hiring Formula – A Dynamic Competency Model

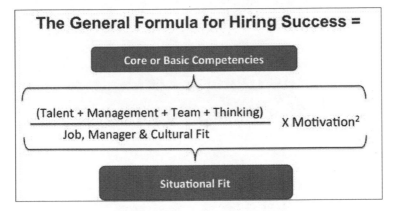

Don't Ignore Fit with the Job, the Manager
and Culture to Assess Motivation

In parallel, over the same past 30 years, I've also been tracking people I've interviewed, placed, and worked with, to see what competencies made them tick, and how these changed over time. Some of these people turned out to be superstars, most were solid and consistent leaders, along with with a few underperformers in the pack. Combining these two separate approaches, I boiled everything into what is I now refer to as The General Formula for Hiring Success. These are the factors shown in the formula.

In simple words, and for definitional purposes, on-the-job success means consistently and successfully getting the job done regardless of the circumstances, with the least direction possible. If a person can do this they have exactly the right level of skills, experience, industry background, and academics needed. Of course, you need to first define on-the-job success before it can be measured. This is why defining the job via the performance profile is so important.

> *In simple words, on-the-job success means consistently and successfully getting the job done regardless of the circumstances with the least direction possible.*

The interviewer can use the hiring formula as a guide for the complete assessment by making sure all of the factors are properly evaluated. While all of the factors shown in the hiring formula are important, extra weight needs to be given to motivation to do the actual work required. But to get motivation right, job fit is critical. These are represented by all of the factors in the bottom of the formula. Doing less than satisfying work, working with a weak manager, or working under very trying circumstances can sap even the most motivated person. The hiring formula has been purposely designed to take fit and motivation into account.

To get started, here's the quick explanation for each term in the hiring formula. Some people call these factors competencies, others call them behaviors. Regardless of what you call them, the idea is that you need to assess them all in order to best predict a person's ability to meet the objectives described in the performance profile. The work-history review and the two-question performance-based interview presented in the next two chapters provide a simple means to accurately assess each of these factors. The core of this is asking candidates to describe major accomplishments comparable to those required for on-the-job success. This is called the Most Significant Accomplishment question (MSA). By digging deep into each accomplishment, the interviewer will gather enough evidence to accurately assess each factor in the formula in comparison to real job needs and the related managerial and cultural circumstances. The second question is called the Problem-solving Question (PSQ) and involves asking candidates how they would figure out how to solve actual job-related problems.

CANDIDATE ADVICE
How to Map Your Success to the Hiring Formula

Think about the specific accomplishments you'd use to best demonstrate your proficiency for each competency shown in the formula. Try to come up with two to three specific examples or projects as part of this preparation. Write down all of the details including your supervisor, the names of the people on the team, the actual dates, your actual role, and the key metrics involved. This is just the beginning, though, since I'm going to suggest that interviewers ask you about every fact imaginable involved in the accomplishment. You won't be able to fake this stuff, either, no matter how eloquent you are. The facts will speak for themselves. So as you read this, start getting prepared. You'll need to know this stuff cold when interviewers start peppering you with questions.

Defining the Traits in the Hiring Formula for Success

Talent is the ability to do the work.

This factor encompasses the level of technical competence and the ability to apply this knowledge to complete tasks and handle job-related challenges. It also includes the ability to learn and apply related technical knowledge. Obviously, some level of technical skills and ability is required to handle just about any job, but many interviewers and hiring managers overdo it. This is most common among those with a technical bent, often demanding brilliance far and above real job needs. While there's no getting around the need for some level of talent and ability, it needs to be measured in terms of real job demands, not some artificial standard imposed by the hiring manager.

In my experience, a solid grasp of the technical demands of the job plus an ability to rapidly learn and apply new knowledge is the right mix. To determine this during the interview you'll need to get specific examples of how the person learned and applied new technical knowledge to get the job done successfully. As part of your assessment, remember that the ability to rapidly learn, apply and execute is a common trait of most high achievers. This is how and why those with less experience can have results similar to those with more experience handling the same types of projects. As a result, they often get promoted more rapidly or get assigned to even bigger projects. All of this is revealed during the work-history review via the Achiever Pattern.

Management is the ability to get the work done on time, properly, and consistently.

For individual contributors this factor focuses on self-management, including time management, organization and planning, discipline, and meeting deadlines on a consistent basis. For team leaders and project managers, it also focuses on organizing teams to achieve consistent, high-quality results. This includes prioritizing and planning work, tracking results, addressing challenges, and obtaining resources. Not making excuses, overcoming obstacles, working under difficult circumstances, and dealing with the resources available is all part of effective management as defined here.

During the interview, ask the candidate to describe a major accomplishment where these types of management skills were critical to job success. Prompt the candidate to give the best examples possible. Questions about tight deadlines, complex issues, and scarce resources should be part of the probing and fact-finding. Ask how the person balanced quality with timeliness. Consistency matters too, so ask about this for multiple accomplishments throughout the person's work history. Find out how tasks and projects were planned and organized, what the results were, how performance was tracked, and whether or not the goal was achieved. The key is to look for a pattern of consistent results in a variety of different situations with different managers. Then compare the complexity and scope of these projects to what the candidate is likely to face on your job.

Team Skills, aka Emotional Intelligence or EQ

EQ refers to the term Daniel Goleman coined in his book, *Emotional Intelligence – Why It Can Matter More Than IQ*. It relates to how the person works with others. Here's his quick definition: "Managing feelings so that they are expressed appropriately and effectively, enabling people to work together smoothly toward their common goals." Goleman describes four major skills that make up emotional intelligence: Self-Awareness, Self-Management, Social Awareness, and Relationship Management. All of these are important, but from the perspective of assessing someone's team skills, I'm mostly concerned with how the person communicates, influences, and works with others, especially on cross-functional project teams. To get a sense of this during the interview, look for examples of how the person interacted on projects and/ or led teams. Seek out coaching examples, dealing with conflict, and persuading or inspiring others. Also look at the make-up of the teams, the person's role, if the team changed or grew in size over time, and if the teams were multi-functional and/or were comprised of senior-level company leaders. Team skills and cultural fit is not determined by warmth or affability during the interview. It's determined by the person's impact and effectiveness in collaborating with others on the teams the person has been asked to join. Leadership is a big part of this, including developing and coaching others, including peers, taking full responsibility for a project's success, and selecting and hiring the team.

As part of the assessment, determine whether the person's team role changed over time. Even better is if this team growth changed with different and credible organizations. Some people always lead, some always follow, and others are flexible enough to accommodate the circumstances to ensure the best team results are achieved. Look for these changing roles. Whatever you discover, the person's team skills need to be assessed in comparison to what's required for the new job. For example, if the person has only worked with accountants for the past five years and your job requires the person to work with operations, logistics, and product marketing to track costs, this could be a challenge for that person. On the other hand, if you have a techie who has been assigned to a variety of different cross-functional teams, you probably have a candidate that understands the needs of other functions. Lack of effective situational team skills leads to underperformance, dissatisfaction, and turnover. This was one of the findings in Google's Project Oxygen study mentioned earlier.

Thinking Skills addresses the person's ability to understand and solve job-related problems.

Good people at every level in an organization, from entry-level customer service reps to seasoned professionals and executives, have the ability to visualize how to accomplish a task or to figure out how to solve a job-related problem. Based on this, they make the best decision. Of course, the scope and complexity of these problems and decisions vary depending on the level and complexity of the job. For some jobs, thinking skills involves planning and determining the resources needed to organize and complete a project. For other jobs, it's figuring out how to solve a problem – technical, team, or otherwise – even uncovering the root cause of the problem. Part of thinking skills involves making trade-offs among competing alternatives and then deciding which is the appropriate course of action.

Many interviewers use "trick" questions to figure out a candidate's thinking and problem-solving ability. There is no evidence that this type of questioning has any predictive value, especially since a good or bad answer is a function of the interviewer's perspective, not a standard benchmark. Regardless, there is plenty of evidence that job-related thinking and problem-solving skills, as defined here, are predictive of on-the-job performance in handling similar problems.[3]

A more valid and predictive way to assess thinking and problem-solving skills involves asking candidates how they would solve or address a specific job-related problem or situation. This is the second of the two core questions in the performance-based interview. The final answer is far less important than the process the person uses to figure out the answer, which is the real purpose of the question. Getting at this involves a back-and-forth dialogue between the interviewer and the candidate.

Toward the end of the problem-solving questioning, ask the person to describe an actual accomplishment that best compares to the problem under discussion. This will validate that the person is not just a good talker, but actually has implemented his/her own advice. This two-question combo is called the Anchor and Visualize (MSA and PSQ combined) interviewing process and is a great means to increase assessment accuracy by getting at both left and right brain competencies. The Problem-solving Question focuses more on right-brain thinking, vision, planning, and creative skills. The anchor accomplishment question focuses more on left-brain performance and analytical skills. Someone who is strong on both, coupled with a track record of comparable performance and the Achiever Pattern, is someone you'll likely want to hire.

Motivation to do the work required is the most important of the factors and also the most difficult to assess.

Some people refer to motivation as drive, self-motivation, persistence, work ethic, or initiative. Regardless of what you call it, it is vitally important for job success. In the formula it's shown as M^2 since it has so much impact on job success, output, and performance. It's also very

---

3   Hunter and Schmidt - *The Validity and Utility of Selection Methods in Personnel Psychology: Practical and Theoretical Implications of 85 Years of Research Findings,* Copyright 1998 by the American Psychological Association, Inc. 0033-2909/98/ S3.00

job specific. Few people are so responsible, committed, disciplined, and self-motivated that they'll be highly motivated doing any type of work in any type of situation. In general, people will go the extra mile doing work they find intellectually or emotionally satisfying under circumstances they find personally satisfying. Assuming basic competency, the below-the-line traits in the formula – job, manager, and cultural fit – are the primary drivers of motivation. During the interview ask about these issues as the candidate describes his/her accomplishments. Then compare these to the actual job and the cultural, team, and managerial issues involved.

To assess motivation properly you need to find multiple examples of where the person went the extra mile doing work comparable to what needs to be done. Alternate terms for motivation could be "drive" or "results-oriented," but the key idea is that during the interview you're not looking for generic motivation, but specific job-related examples of the person doing far more than required. For every MSA question, ask for numerous examples of where the person took the initiative or went the extra mile doing something that was not required. Some people are narrow on this score (e.g., focusing only on technical issues) and others are more broad-based, doing whatever it takes on a project because it was important. Regardless, look for people who are motivated to excel and make sure they'll be equally motivated to do what your job requires. A caveat: get actual examples of going the extra mile recently doing work similar to what your job entails. Also, make sure you ask "when?" these examples took place. You need to find recent examples of motivation to make an accurate comparison. Take generic "I'll do whatever it takes" pronouncements from the candidate with a grain of salt. These are generally based on the need for a job, not from the inner gratification of doing work the person finds truly satisfying.

Job Fit involves determining the person's interest and motivation in doing the actual job.

Ignoring job fit often results in the most common of all hiring mistakes – hiring someone who is competent to do the work, but not motivated to do it. This is why the performance profile is so important. By describing what work needs to be performed, even generically, the interviewer is guided during the interview, always seeking comparable and recent accomplishments of the person doing similar work. Note: the candidate's past accomplishments don't have to be identical; comparable is the key. For example, selling a similar complex product using a similar sales process to a similar buyer, even in a different industry, would be considered comparable. This approach also opens up the pool to a more diverse group of candidates from different industries and backgrounds, including the military.

Managerial Fit addresses the importance of working within the hiring manager's style, the available resources, workload, and the decision-making process.

If the candidate and the hiring manager clash from a style, coaching, and/or development standpoint, the person will fail, regardless of capability. Likewise, if the workload is too demanding, or not demanding enough, or the degree of structure and pace is different than where the candidate has excelled, under-performance is likely. Few interviewers ever fully address this critical aspect of job performance pre-hire, with the expectation that any rough edges can be smoothed out with some type of training program. During the interview ask how decisions and plans were made, the degree of independence the candidate had, and what the resources were like. Also ask about each manager the candidate has worked for to determine whether there's a variation in performance as a result of the manager's style. You'll learn a lot about the candidate's resiliency and character as a result. Some candidates can work with a variety of different managers; others are very narrow. Understanding this breadth is a critical aspect of the assessment process.

Cultural Fit relates to the person meshing with the company's environment, pace, intensity, and its values & mission.

The key problem here is that most people don't know what the company's culture is, but believe they'll know if a person fits it when they meet the person. This is foolhardy. All of this cultural fit can be captured in the performance profile by describing the circumstances, challenges, and environment underlying each of the performance objectives. For example, if there is a need to work with a team of people who are difficult to deal with, this should be captured in the performance profile. During the interview, ask the person to describe the underlying cultural issues as part of the MSA question fact-finding to see if there are any patterns or potential problems.

The above-the-line traits in the formula (those in the numerator) are the generic traits found in most competency models. Review the specific definitions to see how these four factors cover many of the typical competencies like leadership, drive for results, team skills, and curiosity. While these generic traits are appropriate to use as the basis for initial screening, for an accurate assessment they need to be evaluated in context with real job needs and the actual circumstances associated with the job. The latter includes the hiring manager's leadership style, the company culture, and any unusual environmental issues or restraints (e.g., pace is too demanding, inadequate resources, lack of clear expectations).

Hiring cultural misfits is a common and serious problem. This has little to do with personal warmth or team skills. For example, one fast-growing company we've worked with hired a number of talented people, but these new hires were failing since they couldn't adapt to the pace and the lack of resources. One technique to figure this out is to map the person's accomplishment to the company's rate of growth and where it is on the corporate lifecycle (i.e., from start-up to maturity). This is described in detail in the section on making the final assessment.

Using the Hiring Formula for Success to Raise the Talent Bar

Lack of understanding and assessing these below-the-line situational factors (the denominator) turn out to be the most common causes of underperformance and high turnover. If a person doesn't find the work challenging or important (or both), performance will suffer. If the hiring manager's style is not supportive or clashes with how the person needs to be developed, manager and new hire satisfaction will decline with a rise in voluntary turnover. And if you hire cultural misfits, expect failure. The hiring formula for success is pretty simple to understand, but taking shortcuts or making superficial assessments for any of the factors is a formula for disaster.

Aside from improving assessment accuracy, there's a huge, less obvious upside – the hiring formula offers a unique opportunity to expand the candidate pool to include more high potential and diverse candidates, including returning military vets. The hiring formula provides a means to trade off direct skills and experience with some amount of offsetting performance, ability, and potential. If the candidate is a strong fit on all of the non-technical factors and has shown an ability to learn rapidly but is a little light on direct experience, it makes sense to seriously consider the person. There is some balance required when making this potential vs. experience trade-off. As a rule of thumb, I'd suggest as much potential as possible without compromising the need to perform. The less time you have to train the person, the more direct experience is required. As part of this you also have to consider the coaching ability of the hiring manager and related company support and training programs. Regardless, you'll always need to balance the short-term need for execution with the long-term opportunity to hire a top performer as you evaluate potential vs. experience.

Amazon addresses the balancing of skills and experience with potential issue through their Raising the Talent Bar program. Hiring managers in most companies tend to be more concerned with short-term performance rather than achieving the companywide benefit of hiring on potential. At Amazon, an external talent advisory team is involved in each hiring decision to ensure some appropriate balance on this score is achieved. Without this outside-the-department intervention a company's overall talent level is likely to decline rather than increase. Consider a top person making the decision to accept an offer as part of this talent-raising concept. There are a great many managers who are not capable of attracting top performers to work for them. The best people, especially those not looking for lateral transfers, want to work for leaders who can mentor and develop them. Below-average managers have trouble on this score, so some intervention by the hiring manager's manager or the company is needed to ensure the right people are being hired.

Even above-average hiring managers justify their need for "experienced" staff using short-term pressure as an excuse for not investing in long-term talent development. They rationalize this viewpoint by making the weak argument that over-hiring provides the company with the talent needed to handle bigger jobs in the future. Unfortunately, this ignores the flipside: the candidate perspective. There are few top people who are willing to be hired for work that is below their capacity while waiting for the opportunity to demonstrate their abilities. The idea of hiring people this way is not even possible in a talent scarcity situation when the demand for talent exceeds the supply.

The importance of fit can not be overstated. While there are many talented and motivated people around, they can prove to be failures if the circumstances prevent them from being successful. Equally important, there are many apparently average performers who can excel under the right conditions. For example, think about the worst boss you've ever had, or if you've ever taken a job that turned out not to be what was described. If you underperformed in these situations you personally recognize the impact these fit factors can have on your motivation, commitment, and performance. Also consider situations where you excelled, or were totally committed to deliver great results. It could have been the work itself, working on a project or with a team you believed in, or for a supervisor who supported and developed you, and inspired you to go the extra mile. Figuring out the drivers or causal factors behind exceptional work is as important as figuring out the cause of mediocre performance.

During the interview you'll be able to assess the impact these situational fit factors have on candidate performance by asking the person to describe the environment behind each major accomplishment. Patterns will soon emerge. Few people are exceptional under all conditions, under all types of managers, but many exceptional people can continue to be exceptional under the right conditions. You might also find some diamonds in the rough who never had the chance to achieve their full potential. Hiring these people and converting them into all-stars is the stuff of high-potential managerial dreams. It can never happen by narrowing your focus to matching on skills, experience, and industry background.

Understanding the impact of these situational fit factors is part of preparing a complete performance profile. During the assessment you'll compare the actual work the person has done and the environment in which it was done to what's described in the performance profile. This will ensure that the below-the-line performance maps directly to the above-the-line competencies. Even better, you'll stop hiring people who were stars under different circumstances and start hiring more people who have demonstrated they can thrive in your environment, even if they have a slightly different background than what's described in the traditional job description.

CANDIDATE ADVICE
How to Use the Hiring Formula as a Framework for Presenting Yourself

There's a full chapter later in this book about how to properly prepare and present yourself for the interview. One idea discussed, and the core theme of this book, is the need to provide examples of your major accomplishments and significant work projects as part of your responses to an interviewer's question. These examples, especially if they're in specific detail, and only if they're relevant, are valued more highly by most interviewers than generic, lofty, or verbose statements.

There is a tendency on the part of many interviewers to ask trick questions, use intuition or some other unscientific means to determine competency, motivation, and fit. This is not all their fault. Most interviewers don't know what they're looking for in terms of actual job needs. Most have never been exposed to anything like the hiring formula, and even fewer have ever thought of getting multiple examples of accomplishments to assess each of the traits. Given the actual state of interviewing skills possessed by most managers, the use of trick questions, intuition, and "un-science" is a logical, albeit flawed, consequence. Of course, none of these things predict a person's on-the-job performance. So in addition to being a waste of time, they also result in many good candidates being excluded for bad reasons, and weaker candidates often being hired instead.

As a candidate you can't let the interviewer assess you using these techniques. You'll be judged unfairly if you don't intercede. If you've ever been judged this way and didn't get a job offer, you're familiar with one side of the consequence of this method. If you got the job and it turned out not to be what you thought, you've experienced the other side. Neither outcome is a good one. It's much better to be evaluated based on what you've accomplished. A rejection based on sound evidence is certainly better than being rejected or accepted for cosmetic or superficial reasons. Getting an offer based on what you've accomplished is the goal. Knowing this, you'll be able to use this approach to make sure you're judged fairly regardless of the interviewer's competence. As a result, don't be surprised as you become a legitimate contender for a lot more jobs than you initially imagined.

There are two parts to improving your odds of getting an offer for a job you deserve. One is getting the interviewer to ask the right questions; two is answering the questions correctly. In the prepping for the interview chapter, I'll describe a simple technique to get the hiring managers to ask you the right questions. Getting ready to answer the question is more challenging, and the hiring formula can help you prepare your accomplishment-based answers.

First go through each of your past jobs and list all of the big accomplishments. These could be team or individual projects you led or in which you had a key role. Prepare a short one-paragraph overview of the project including the dates, the company, your title, your specific role, and how you got assigned to the project. Then look at the hiring formula and add details for each of the traits listed. Be specific with these. Emphasize those traits that helped you succeed in the role. For example, saying you led a small technical team in 2009 consisting of manufacturing, engineering, and accounting to overcome some complex manufacturing challenges when launching a new project that saved your company $1.8mm in start-up costs, is a lot better than saying you're a problem-solver. Write all of this information down for every single accomplishment. It might take a few hours to put it all together, but it will all be important when it comes to the interview, even if you don't use it all at once.

How you use this information is important. For one thing, don't just parrot this stuff back like an automaton. Instead, parse segments into your responses to the interviewers in some logical, appropriate, and relevant way. If the interviewer's questions are unfair, ask the interviewer to describe some of the key challenges involved in the job. If they're looking for some of the things you've accomplished, mention the more relevant accomplishments. Don't get into too many details right away. Provide just enough for a minute or two to excite the interviewer, with the hope you'll entice the person to ask for more information.

The idea behind this is akin to a sales technique called solution selling. In this process, the role of the sales person is to uncover the customers' needs or problems, and then offer a solution. A good candidate needs to do something similar if he/she wants to be judged fairly. It starts by being prepared to discuss your accomplishments in any depth needed. Being prepared gives you the confidence you need to make sure the interviewer is asking you the right questions. If not, you won't be able to figure out what the actual open job is all about, and offer yourself as the best solution. As you go through the next chapter on interviewing, you'll find out what hiring managers should be asking you, but if you prepare as described above, you'll have no problems being assessed properly. The key is to get the interviewer to ask you the right questions.

Summary – Understanding and Using the Hiring Formula for Success

- The General Formula for Hiring Success offers a simple means to assess candidate competency across all job factors. In simple terms, hiring success is equal to overall ability in comparison to job fit, multiplied by motivation squared. Ability includes technical competency, execution, team skills, and problem solving. Fit addresses the actual job, the company culture, and the manager's style. Matching ability to these fit factors is essential since collectively it drives motivation. Without the right fit, even great people will underperform.

- The hiring formula offers a means to make the trade-off between skills and experience, and potential and performance. Too many managers over-emphasize the short-term needs of the job minimizing the organizational need to continually raise the overall talent level of the company. Those with a track record of achievement and high performance in comparable situations are highly likely to perform at peak levels, even if their mix of skills and experience is different or lighter than specified in the job description. This is an important issue to consider especially when implementing diversity or military recruiting programs.

- Candidates can use the hiring formula to prepare for the interview. The idea is to write down accomplishments that best demonstrate their actual competency for each of the factors in the formula. The accomplishments need to be as detailed as possible, including specific details, dates, and results. This is important since few interviewers consider generic statements about ability when making their subsequent assessments. However, these same interviewers do use specific examples of accomplishments as a means to reach their conclusions about whether to hire a candidate.

Chapter 3

Interviewing: Work-History Review and the Achiever Pattern

Conducting a professional and thorough interview is at the core of making the right hiring decision. Everyone who has input into the hiring decision needs to be able to do this well. Good candidates expect a complete and thorough interview. In fact, they'll use the quality and depth of the interview to make a judgment about the company, the hiring manager, the recruiter, the hiring team, and the quality of its hiring standards. Good people don't mind earning the right to be hired, as long as the right information is being measured the right way.

The Primary Purposes of the Interview

1) Accurately assess competency and motivation to do the work required.

2) Send a message to the candidate that the company and interviewer have high hiring standards.

3) Clarify job expectations, without overselling or being long-winded.

4) Get the candidate to see that the job offers a true career move.

5) Negotiate the offer in a series of steps, rather than waiting until the end of the assessment process.

....

If you've ever been a candidate you know that most interviewers haven't done a very good job of assessing you. Many overvalue first impressions, some trust their intuition more than others, and others consider technical brilliance as the "be all, end all." You might even have been a little nervous, and didn't answer the questions as well as you would have liked. This is the collective summary of all the problems shown in the hiring flow chart graphic in the previous chapter highlighting the four time-phased decision points, including Moment 1.

The Interview is More Than an Assessment Tool

Few managers take the time to fully understand their real job requirements, and as a result, can't accurately determine whether the candidate is both motivated and competent to do the work required in the actual environment of the job. Without knowing real job requirements the assessment will be made on something other than competency and motivation to do the actual work in the actual situation.

The Performance-based Hiring process starts by first defining on-the-job success by creating a performance profile. Chapter 6 is entirely devoted to preparing these, but simply put, a performance profile lists the top 5-6 things the person needs to do well in order to be considered at least a B+ or better performer. Without the performance profile as a benchmark, making an accurate assessment is not possible, since you're not evaluating the person in the context of the actual work that needs to be done or the unique circumstances involved. Circumstances in this case referring to the people involved, the company culture, the resources available, and the actual environment.

CANDIDATE ADVICE
Ask the Right Kind of Questions

If you're reading this chapter from a candidate perspective, you'll discover there are many things you can do to make sure that you're being evaluated properly against real job needs. Part of this is asking appropriate questions during the interview to steer the interviewer in the right direction. I'll highlight these points as they come up, but it's important to make a note of what you can do to control the types of questions being asked.

If you're on the hiring side of the table, put yourself in the candidate's shoes and think how you would answer the same questions. This will help you better understand the real purpose of the interview and appreciate the give-and-take process being described. Then when you do become a candidate – which everyone eventually becomes – you'll know exactly what to do even if the interviewer doesn't.

There are multiple stages in the assessment process from phone screening to full onsite interviews spanning multiple sessions and multiple interviewers. As shown above, interviewing involves much more than just assessing the candidate. There is a lot of recruiting that goes on in the interview. Part of this relates to the quality, rigor, and depth of the interview. Candidates are deeply affected by this.

Too many hiring managers think they can save the recruiting component until they've decided to hire someone. This will backfire, especially with passive candidates, but even active candidates may require one or two exploratory conversations before the full assessment process can begin. Most people, especially those who aren't actively looking and those with multiple opportunities, want to understand more about the company and the job before becoming too serious. Part of this is learning something about the hiring manager's leadership qualities and management style. Along with handling these variations in candidate needs, knowing how to interview well should be a prerequisite for every manager.

Over the past 20 years I've developed a rather simple interviewing process that involves an in-depth work-history review and just two core interview questions. As you'll soon discover, this performance-based interviewing process can be used to measure every aspect of on-the-job performance including all of the factors in the hiring formula. It can also be easily modified whether the candidate is anxious to proceed or wants to know a lot more before committing.

Overview of the Performance-based Interviewing Process

The performance-based interviewing approach described in this book covers a number of basic steps. Here's a general outline of the process with links to the appropriate sections:

- **Prepare a performance-based job description to replace the traditional skills- and experience-based job description.** This is the performance profile. It lists the primary performances objectives of the position. A performance profile describes what the person in the role needs to do to be considered successful, not what the person needs to have in terms of skills and experiences. Preparing performance profiles is covered in Chapter 6.

• **Conduct an exploratory phone screen.** A 30-minute phone interview starts by reviewing the candidate's LinkedIn profile or resume, and conducting a basic Work-history review. Part of this is looking for the Achiever Pattern, indicating the person is in the top 25% of his/her peer group. If the candidate is a reasonable fit, the interviewer should ask the Major Accomplishment Question (MSA) for the most important performance objective in the performance profile. Based on this, the interviewer will be able to determine if the candidate should be recommended for a more complete interview.

• **Prepare a preliminary assessment using the Quality of Hire Talent Scorecard.** A copy of the scorecard is in the appendix and described in-depth in Chapter 5. The scorecard is divided into three sections: Basic Skills and the Achiever Pattern, the Core Competencies in the Hiring Formula for Success, and the Situational Fit Factors in the formula. After the phone screen it's possible to make a reasonable decision if a full interview is appropriate.

• **Conduct the Performance-based Interview.** A copy of the complete eight-step Performance-based Interview is in the Appendix. The bulk of this involves conducting a Work-history review and asking the two basic questions – the MSA question and the Problem-solving Question (PSQ). The MSA question is used to assess the candidate's past performance in comparison to the performance objectives in the performance profile. The PSQ is used to determine if the candidate has the problem-solving, thinking and decision-making skills required for on-the-job success. Other steps in the interview process include the opening setup, techniques to maintain objectivity, and recruiting and closing.

- **Organize the interview for multiple interviewers.** Organizing the interview properly helps increase assessment accuracy. A tool has been provided in Chapter 5 to help assign each interviewer specific areas in the hiring formula to focus upon. While each interviewer will use the same performance-based questioning approach, by narrowing their focus, their understanding of the factors they're responsible for will increase.

- **Conduct a complete evidence-based assessment using the Quality of Hire Talent Scorecard.** The factors shown on the talent scorecard map directly to those in the hiring formula. To assess these properly, a formal debriefing process is essential. As part of this each interviewer will present the evidence they used to rank the candidate on the 1-5 scale on the scorecard. By sharing evidence this way, on a factor-by-factor basis, the overall accuracy of the assessment increases dramatically.

The Work-History Review

Most interviewers don't fully appreciate the situational issues (i.e., actual job, hiring manager's style, unusual circumstances, company culture, and the environment) associated with the job. A poor match on any of these is typically the reason otherwise good people underperform. This is also why someone possessing all of the skills and experiences listed in the job description isn't necessarily going to be a top performer. Equally important, we've all met people who have performed well without the full complement of the skills and experiences listed. Consider those people who get promoted at your company as part of this latter group. Lack of direct experience and an absolute level of skills is not a good predictor of capability. That's why it's so critical not to use "Before

Day 1" criteria to eliminate candidates, especially diverse candidates and returning military vets. If a candidate is reasonably close, I suggest substituting achievement and potential for any deficiency in skills and experience. You'll be able to figure much of this out in the first 20-30 minutes of the interview during the work-history review.

Whether you're phone screening the person or conducting a full interview, I suggest you start with an in-depth work-history review. This puts a great framework around the person. It's very difficult to make an objective assessment without a solid knowledge of the person's work-history and why he or she took different positions and how well they performed in these jobs. You can use a resume or the person's LinkedIn profile for this review. Focus the assessment on basic fit, the level of skills, overall performance, and upside potential. Here are the big steps involved in conducting a work-history review:

- **Review the past 5-10 years with the focus on years and titles.** This will give you a general sense of the person's overall fit with the job, the comparability of the companies and industries, and a rough idea if the person is progressing appropriately in his or her career. Of course, you should modify how much work history to evaluate depending on the level of the job.

- **Ask about major projects and accomplishments.** For each job find out about the biggest projects led or changes implemented. Scope this out in terms of budget, team size, overall impact, and importance. You'll ask about some of these projects later if you decide the candidate is a reasonable fit and if it's worth conducting a more in-depth interview.

- **Build 360° work charts.** Ask about the person's organization including who he/she reported to and who reported to them. Also ask about project teams the person was on and who was on the teams. The best people are assigned to cross-functional teams earlier than normal. The size and importance of these teams is an indicator of both team and leadership skills, influence, and potential.

- **Have the person explain gaps in employment.** Don't assume the worst – poor performance. Significant gaps between jobs could be due to bad economic times or a very appropriate personal decision, like raising a family. Regardless, it's important to understand why the person left or lost a job and how they went about finding a new one. Look for resiliency, persistence, and self-development. Avoid constant excuse-making. If the gaps are lengthy expect the person to have proactively become better at something through formal training.

- **Have the person explain job changes.** Self-initiated job changes are very revealing. Understand why and how the person went from one company to another. Then find out if the person accomplished the purpose for the change. Many people leave jobs for superficial reasons and accept offers without conducting appropriate due diligence. Lack of progression is a clue this is the case. The best people leave jobs for lack of career opportunities and get them in their subsequent roles.

- **Highlight all promotions.** The strongest people get promoted, either being assigned to bigger or more important projects, or to lead teams. Find out if there is a pattern to this and what the person accomplished to get them. Most likely it was strong technical skills, but it's better if the person had strong team and project management skills.

- **Look for continuous recognition.** For each job ask if the person received some type of formal recognition. A promotion is obvious. Being assigned to lead or be part of an important project requires some digging. Sales people always get obvious rewards, but for professional staff it takes some clever probing to find out. The best technical people get assigned the toughest technical problems early in their careers. Some people get awarded fellowships or receive unusual training opportunities; others write white papers or speak at industry conferences.

- **Look for "patterns of success."** If the person has been in the workforce more than five years, you'll start observing patterns of doing work that are repeated year after year. It could be how the person uncovers problems and implements change, or how the person turns around an organization, or how he or she builds and manages teams. Be concerned if there is a lack of consistency, and become excited when you see it.

- **Diversity of experience, environments, and circumstances.** Zoom out and determine whether there is an obvious connection among the person's jobs. This could be the industry, the size of the companies and their growth rates, the types of managers the person worked for, and the types of people the person has hired. Be concerned if this range is narrow, especially if the environments where the person excelled are different than your company's situation. On the other hand, be open-minded if the person seems to excel in a variety of circumstances. Too many interviewers exclude people who are from different companies and similar industries. Being able to succeed in a variety of situations is more important. This indicates flexibility and upside potential.

Focus on the traits in the hiring formula as you're conducting the work-history review. This will help guide your fact-finding around each job. Pay particular attention to the situational fit factors. Getting these right is as important as assessing skills and experiences. If the person is a reasonable fit for the job it's obvious you'd want to continue the interview. Don't be a box-checker, though. Reasonable fit does not mean perfect fit. The person doesn't have to be from the same industry or the same type of company as long as the work being done is comparable in complexity and the situational fit factors are close. In fact, if the person is a bit light on skills and experience, but heavy on potential, you absolutely must consider the candidate.

CANDIDATE ADVICE
Handling the Work-History Review

Don't screen yourself out if you see a job posting that isn't a perfect fit. But if you expect to get an interview and get past the first screen, you'd better demonstrate some extraordinary strengths on one or two of the factors described above. To get started, review each of the work-history review factors in detail and be prepared to discuss them all in depth without prompting or evasiveness. A number of reasonable examples for each will often suffice. Emphasize those areas that you believe are your strengths. You must provide evidence in the form of external recognition for these. Generalizations and hyperbole will not suffice. If some of your strengths are not brought up naturally as part of the interview, you can force the issue. Just ask the hiring manager if the factor is important for on-the job success. Then make your case. For example, if coaching and mentoring others is a common theme of your work history, force the point via a question if the interviewer overlooks this. As a candidate your first task is not to get an offer, it's to be invited back for another round of interviews. To do this, you must demonstrate that your work history is a strong fit, especially if it's not obvious.

Later in this book I'll be introducing our Quality of Hire Talent Scorecard. This tool provides a formal means to evaluate the candidate on all of the factors in the hiring formula plus a method to make the trade-off between skills and experience and potential. The key to this trade-off is to look for the Achiever Pattern as you're conducting the work-history review. The Achiever Pattern indicates that the person is in the top-half of the top-half of his or her peer group. This is the top 25% and includes evidence like rapid promotions, being assigned to critical and/or multi-functional teams, or being asked to lead, coach, train, or mentor others. You'll be able to obtain all of this information if you conduct the work-history review as described. Most high-potential candidates exhibit this pattern very early in their careers and carry it consistently throughout. If you spot this, be less concerned if the person is a bit light in years of experience or direct background. Instead consider the fact that the person has been formally recognized because of their exceptional performance. Hiring these people is how you raise your company's overall talent level.

The Achiever Pattern

Top people always get recognized, somehow. Sometimes this recognition is obvious, like an early promotion or special award or bonus, or being assigned to the toughest client or the most difficult technical challenge. For example, great sales people become President's Club members and attend the annual offsite in Hawaii. Sometimes top people are provided fellowships for graduate study at a prestigious university or are asked to lead a special high-visibility project. Sometimes the recognition is less obvious, but still real. For example, an engineer being assigned to a cross-functional team or an accountant being asked to help design and implement a major new business system would be recognition that the person is being acknowledged for doing great work. This type of recognition is collectively referred to as the Achiever Pattern. People in the top 25% of their peer group have lots of this type of recognition. As you begin any phone screen or interview you should be looking for this. Often you'll have to dig for it.

THE ACHIEVER PATTERN

1) Track record of consistent upward progress.

2) Formal recognition for doing exceptional work.

3) Assigned to bigger projects or special roles earlier than expected.

4) Rapid promotions, special rewards, or unusual bonuses.

5) Working on cross-functional teams, with company executives, or those outside the company on critical issues.

6) Being involved in big decisions that wouldn't normally be assigned to someone at the person's level.

....

In my opinion, I wouldn't recommend or hire someone who doesn't possess the Achiever Pattern. Here are some things to look for as evidence the person possesses it:

- **Promotions are good, but promotions faster than the norm are even better.** Even better still are consistent promotions at multiple, different, and credible organizations.

- **If the person was rehired by a former boss it indicates someone else recognized the person for his or her ability to perform.** If the candidate hired some top people from a former company it indicates that the person is a strong manager who can attract and develop other strong people.

- **Assigned to handle the toughest problems.** These could be technical, working with difficult or important customers, or being asked to work on important company initiatives.

- **A track record of working with bigger, more diverse groups.** Working on multi-functional teams early in a person's career is a sure sign the person has been recognized for thinking beyond the functional requirements of the job. If these teams also consist of working with more senior executives and customers, all the better.

- **Being assigned to process-improvement programs or long-range planning committees.** Find out why and how the person got assigned and what role the person played. It could be due to their exceptional technical expertise or their ability to implement change. Both are important. If the person was assigned to the team to address long-term strategic issues, especially multi-functional in nature, it's a clue others think the person can understand cause-and-effect and see beyond day-to-day business issues.

- **Find out if the person ever made some type of presentation to senior management.** Good people get this opportunity early in their career.

- **Receiving awards, honors, or special recognition programs.** Some of these are obligatory, but others offer insight that the person has done something far beyond the norm. Receiving these regularly and recently in different circumstances is an important indicator that the person was, and still is, an Achiever.

- **Advanced educational opportunities.** Few companies will invest in their employees' development beyond the norm, unless they believe the person is worth the investment. Winning a work-study fellowship at a prestigious graduate school is an important indicator the person is someone special. Find out what happened to the person when they got back to the company to see how they took advantage of the opportunity given to them.

If you're a hiring manager I urge you to meet people who are high on potential but are a bit light on experience. You might have to adjust the job to better fit their needs, but these are the people who will likely become the future leaders of your company. If you're a recruiter, don't quickly dismiss people who don't meet the skills and experience requirements listed on the job description. You might have to urge your hiring managers to meet these people, but it will be worth the effort.

While evidence of the Achiever Pattern is important, it's not sufficient. The person still needs to meet all of the other standards of excellence described in the hiring formula. Lack of congruity between the two, however, should raise the caution flag. Regardless, possessing the Achiever Pattern is an important indicator you're dealing with a top-notch person. If a person doesn't possess it, at least to some degree, caution is urged.

CANDIDATE ADVICE
Presenting Your Achiever Pattern

The Achiever Pattern is important. If you have it, make sure you summarize all of the recognition you've received and make sure it's visible on your resume and LinkedIn profile. If your pattern is not as broad as you'd like, emphasize those areas where you have been recognized for extraordinary effort. Then seek out situations in the open job where this is important. You'll do this by asking the interviewer about specific challenges that the new hire will face. For example, if you can solve tough production-yield problems because you're tenacious, ask if this type of effort is important for job success. Working on high-performing teams is a component of the Achiever Pattern, so ask about this, too. If you've been on these types of teams, describe the project in detail, how you got on the team, and what your role was in bringing the project to a successful conclusion. Details are an important part of your answer to any question. Embedding these details with evidence of the Achiever Pattern is more important.

Many (probably most) interviewers won't ask you about this recognition as described here. In that case, you need to bring it up in some subtle way. Asking the interviewer to describe some of the challenges in the job will allow you to give some examples of your accomplishments in this area. As you're explaining this, mention how you were recognized. This can be said naturally, and adds a lot of credibility to your story. Of course, don't ask about these challenges if you don't have any relevant accomplishments to brag about. (If you needed this cautionary advice, it's probably best you thoroughly reread the section on Preparing for the Interview before your next interview.)

Look for a Track Record of Consistent B+ Performance

In addition to this Achiever Pattern, another better predictor of success than an absolute level of skills and experiences is having a consistent track record of past B+ performance doing somewhat comparable work under similar circumstances. In this case comparable could be 75-85% of the skills and experiences in environments that are the same, even if the industries aren't identical. If you've ever personally been promoted into a bigger job with a different set of challenges, and have been successful, or know someone who has, you've experienced this approach first hand. It also demonstrates the point that you don't need all of the skills and experiences listed to be successful; you just need to be a top performer in a variety of comparable situations. This goes back to the point made earlier about hiring high potential candidates who have a different mix of skills or are light in overall experience. This is how you raise your talent level, but in these cases, the hiring manager needs to be willing to coach or support a top person through this extra learning phase.

Although noble in concept, hiring someone lighter is not always the best idea, at least if you have a critical project coupled with some severe time restraints. In this case you'll need someone who has been through this type of challenge before. But even in this case, I'd be more comfortable with someone who has demonstrated their ability to rise to the occasion rather than someone who has an overabundance of skills and experiences.

With the idea of making a "skills and experience" vs. "performance and potential" tradeoff as an option, I suggest that each interview begins by first looking for the Achiever Pattern rather than the more typical approach of box-checking off the laundry list of skills and required experience. Worst case, you'll want to put the person on the front-burner for something else if the gap is too big. Best case, you'll modify the job at hand or create another one that best fits the person's capabilities. None of this is even possible if you screen first on skills and experience exclusively or the person opts out without a full understanding of what opportunities and options are available.

As a side note, which will be discussed in more depth later, this tradeoff approach might be one way to open up your talent pool to military vets, diverse candidates, and those reentering the workforce, without compromising on potential or performance. The idea here is that if the skills and experience gap is too big for the manager to handle through on-the-job coaching, the company might need to intervene in some formal way with additional training. This might even involve developing supporting programs with outside trade schools and colleges designed to meet specific company needs.

Summary – Interviewing: Work-History Review and the Achiever Pattern

- **The interview is more than an assessment tool.** Of course, you need to accurately assess candidate competency and motivation to do the work you want done, but too many interviewers don't appreciate the broader implications of effective interviewing. For one thing, an in-depth interview sends a powerful message to all candidates that your company has high standards. For another, it's a great way to clarify expectations upfront and get the candidate excited about the career opportunities inherent in the position without overselling.

- **Recognize the importance of the Achiever Pattern.**
The best people in any field get bigger rewards, receive formal recognition, get assigned tougher projects, win awards, speak at conferences, are assigned to multi-functional teams, and get promoted more rapidly, among other things. Collectively this is the Achiever Pattern indicating the person is in the top-half of the top-half. Look for this pattern when evaluating candidates. These high-achievers often don't have the exact skills needed for the job, but they represent the future success of your company.

- **Look for a track record of consistent B+ performance.**
When in doubt about a candidate, look for consistent performance in a variety of different situations. Solid performers who are flexible, can work successfully with a wide variety of managers, always deliver, rarely make excuses, and can be counted upon regardless of the challenge, represent the manager's dream hire. However, they often don't have stellar resumes or perfect presentation skills. An in-depth work-history review provides important clues to consistent performance as well as the lack of it.

- **Candidates and the Work-History Review.** Don't minimize the importance of the work-history review. This is make-or-break time. Your goal is to get to the next step: a full assessment. The jobs you're fully qualified for might not be the best jobs, so don't cut yourself short. If you're interviewing for a job that's a bit different or bigger, make sure you can relate your experiences and skills to the company's needs. Highlight your strengths that might not be clear in the typical work-history review. Provide evidence of the Achiever Pattern if it's hidden. Most important, make sure you demonstrate consistent and successful performance in a variety of business situations, especially if they're a bit different than the job description.

Chapter 4

The Two-Question Performance-based Interview

Over many years I've developed two questions that can be used to assess a candidate on each of the factors in the general formula for hiring success. When these two questions are combined with good recruiting skills and a performance profile defining exceptional performance, all of the typical problems with accurately assessing a person are overcome. Even better, the candidate is provided with all of the information needed to make a balanced career decision. I call these questions the "Anchor and Visualize" pattern.

The First Question: Tell me about your Most Significant Accomplishment (MSA)

The first question involves asking candidates to describe a significant business accomplishment related to an actual performance objective required for job success. Most jobs have 5-6 performance objectives that collectively represent top performance. These documents are referred to as performance profiles, and I'll describe how to prepare these for any job in Chapter 6. Typically each performance objective takes this form: "Build a marketing team to launch the new series of software apps by Q3," or "Make 10 formal presentations per month to C-level officers as the most critical aspect of our sales process." These performance objectives are action-oriented and cover all aspects of on-the-job success.

Once you know what great performance looks like via the performance profile, all you need to do is ask the candidate to give you an example of something significant he/she has done that's most comparable. The MSA question needs to be asked for each performance objective in the performance profile, although these can be assigned to the different interviewers on the hiring team. As an example for the first objective listed above, the form of the question might be, "We need to launch a complete series of new business software applications over the next six months. This is under a very tight schedule with limited advertising resources. Can you tell me about some major accomplishment you've led that's most comparable?"

The fact-finding that follows is the key to obtaining a complete answer. One way to do this is to ask "SMARTe" fact-finding questions for clarifying the accomplishment. After the candidate gives you a 1-2 minute overview of the comparable accomplishment, ask the following:

- **S**pecific task: Can you please describe the task, challenge, project, or problem?

- **M**easurable: What actually changed, or can you measure your performance somehow?

- **A**ction: What did you actually do and what was your specific role?

- **R**esult: What was the actual result achieved and/or what was the deliverable?

- **T**imeframe: When did this take place and how long did it take?

- **e**nvironment: What was the environment like in terms of pace, resources, level of sophistication, the people involved, and your manager?

FACT-FINDING PROBES TO PEEL THE ONION

- What was your exact role?
- When did it take place?
- Walk me through the plan and the results.
- Give me some examples of initiative.
- Walk me through the biggest decision made.
- Who was on the team? What was your role?
- What was the biggest challenge?
- Describe your supervisor's style.
- Did your supervisor help or hinder? How?
- What was the biggest problem you faced?
- How did you overcome the problem?
- What would you do differently if you could?
- How did you grow as a result of this?
- Were there any lessons learned?
- What was the biggest mistake you made?
- What was the environment like?
- What did you like most and least?
- What did you learn the most?
- What type of recognition did you receive?

While this covers only a small portion of the fact-finding possibilities, using just this SMARTe list will give you a deeper sense of the accomplishment and how it compares to the performance profile. To increase your understanding of the accomplishment, get specific examples for each of these SMARTe fact-finding questions by asking, "Can you give me a specific example of what you mean?" It typically takes 10-15 minutes "peeling the onion" this way to totally understand the accomplishment.

Uncover the Core and Situational Factors
Driving Every Accomplishment

You can use this same fact-finding approach if you want to laser focus on any of the factors in the hiring formula. For example, if you're interested in team skills just ask the candidate to tell you who was involved in the project, the role they played, the candidate's actual role, and how the candidate interacted with these team members. Ask for examples of how the person dealt with conflict or where the person had to persuade or influence people in an important way. The major accomplishment graphic emphasizes the point that it takes multiple traits to achieve meaningful results.

The purpose of detailed fact-finding is to paint a complete word-picture of the person's past comparable accomplishments in order to assess their ability to handle the actual requirements of the new job. The fact-finding approach allows the interviewer to "reverse engineer" the person's accomplishment, and in the process find out not only what the person really did, but how it was done, and what the circumstances were like. This is why each of these MSA questions can take 15 minutes or more to fully understand and appreciate what the candidate actually accomplished.

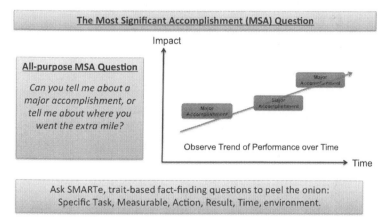

The Trend Line of Major Accomplishment Reveals Growth and Consistency

During a full interview you'll ask a number of different MSA questions covering an extended period of time, at least 5-10 years, maybe more for those who have been in the workforce longer.

As shown in the graph, trending these major accomplishments allow you to observe the person's growth over time.

While upward progression is a positive sign – and typical of those possessing a strong Achiever Pattern – it's not a prerequisite for hiring someone. A line that slopes upward initially and then flattens, while of initial concern, could be a positive if the person continues to do outstanding work. This must be validated, of course. A downward slope if temporary, and/or of short duration, could be attributed more to circumstances than a lack of motivation or ability. Regardless, it's essential to fully understand this issue. Make sure you ask a series of MSA questions and examine the person's progression over time. The direction and slope of the line are very revealing. From an assessment standpoint, you'll need to compare the trend of these accomplishments to the performance profile in order to ensure job fit.

Comparing Performance-based Interviewing with Behavioral Interviewing

This trending approach is one of the fundamental differences between performance-based interviewing and traditional behavioral interviewing. Recognize that the trend of performance is as important, if not more so, than each individual accomplishment. This concept is not even considered in behavioral interviewing. I have a few other big problems with traditional behavioral interviewing (aka Behavioral Event Interviewing or BEI) which are important to clarify:

1) BEI is based on the idea of asking candidates to provide a reasonable example of something they've done that best represents a competency, skill, or behavior. To better understand this interviewers are trained to ask STAR-like (Situation, Task, Action, Result) follow-up questions. For example, here is a typical question: "Can you tell me about a time when you demonstrated dealing with conflict?" The problem I have with this basic approach is that one example is not enough to see a trend, and the example chosen by the candidate might not relate to the job at hand. Worse, it might not even relate to the performance needs of the job. This flaw is eliminated when these same questions are asked as a subset of the MSA question as part of the fact-finding.

2) Candidates can fake BEI questions. Every person on the planet can come up with 3-4 examples of each of the factors in the formula for success. There are books written on how to do this and any savvy interviewer has read them. What they can't do is fake how they used these traits to accomplish tasks most comparable to the real job needs listed in the performance profile. After fact-finding for 10-15 minutes around a single accomplishment you'll know if the story holds true, and the candidate's exact role.

CANDIDATE ADVICE
Do Your Homework to Get a Job You Deserve

Do your homework as described in Chapter 2. This book is not written to help you get jobs you don't deserve. It's written to help you get jobs you do deserve by making sure you're being assessed properly.

The Second Question: How would you solve this problem?

The MSA questions represent the candidate's best examples of comparable past performance in relation to actual job requirements. The second question uncovers another dimension of performance, including job-related problem-solving skills, decision-making, creativity, planning, strategic and multi-functional thinking, and potential. This question is called the Problem-solving Question, or PSQ. Using the above example, the form of this question would be, "If you were to get this job, what would you need to know or do to ensure the product launch was handled successfully?" Based on the person's response, get into a back-and-forth dialogue asking about how he/she would put a plan together, determine resources needed, uncover potential problems, compare alternatives, decide which course of action is best, and prioritize activities.

The Problem-Solving Question

Describe a legitimate job-related problem, and ask the candidate how he/she would solve it. Here are some follow-up questions to ask as part of a back-and-forth dialogue:

1) What would you do first?
2) How would you determine the resources needed?
3) Whose advice would you seek out?
4) How would you determine the root cause?
5) How would you prioritize the work?
6) How would you compare alternatives?
7) How long do you think it would take and how would you figure this out?
8) How would you conduct the cost-benefit evaluation of the alternatives available?
9) What do you think the biggest challenges would be in implementing the solution chosen?
10) How would you decide the best approach?
11) ANCHOR: What have you done that's most similar?

....

In practice, you wouldn't need to ask this second question for every performance objective in the performance profile – just the most critical ones. After trying this question out a few times, you'll discover that the best people quickly obtain a clear understanding of the project or problem by asking appropriate questions and offer different ideas about how to proceed. Based on this, you'll be able to ascertain if the person can put together a reasonable go-forward plan of action based on a thorough understanding of the problem. I'd urge caution if the person gave a detailed response without full consideration and understanding of the differences at your company, including the resources available, the culture, and the challenges involved.

Note: the purpose of this question and subsequent back-and-forth dialogue is to uncover thinking and problem-solving skills, not to determine whether the person's approach is right or wrong. This is not a consulting project. It's the process of figuring out a solution that you're assessing. We'll dig more into assessing the response in the chapter on making the actual assessment, but here are the things you'll be looking for to evaluate the quality of the candidate's responses:

1) The quality and insight of the person's questions in figuring out the real problem and determining the company's range of options.

2) The clarity of the person's approach and plan of action. Good people know how to figure out a problem even if they haven't done the exact same thing before.

3) Be concerned if the answers are vague and general. If the person doesn't even know how to start by asking the right questions, it's hard to believe they'll do anything differently once on the job.

4) The variety of options considered should go beyond what the candidate already knows. Seeking outside advice is part of this and the quality of who the candidate would contact needs to be part of the assessment. Only presenting narrow, internal approaches is a caution flag. You want to hire people who can consider all options and the insight of others given realistic constraints, like limited budget, time, or resources, to get the problem solved successfully.

Here are some examples of job-related PSQs:

1) *We have a tight schedule for the project but don't want to sacrifice quality to meet the deadline. What would you need to know to figure out how to make this trade-off?*

2) *We have high turnover in the sales group. The new manager needs to address this right away and figure out how to minimize the problem. How would you start?*

3) *We've just uncovered a major technical glitch testing the new product. If we don't resolve it quickly it will have a huge impact on product costs and the delivery schedule. This will be the first thing the new hire focuses on. Walk me through your approach to addressing this critical issue.*

The Anchor and Visualize Pattern

There are a few caveats to consider when asking the Problem-solving Question. First, the problem must be job-related. Second, overreliance on this type of question can result in hiring someone who can talk a good game but can't deliver the results. Execution is as important as problem-solving and planning. While being able to visualize a solution to the problem or task is a critical component of exceptional performance, it's only part of the solution. Accomplishing the task successfully is the other part.

Many bright people, including those who are inexperienced, can eloquently and insightfully describe how they'd figure out a problem and suggest a meaningful course of action. However, if they haven't done anything even reasonably comparable in scope, it's questionable if they'll be successful without lots of support. Emphasizing thinking skills over actual past performance is the primary cause of hiring people who are partially competent. These are the people who are good at planning and strategizing, but not so good at executing and delivering. To eliminate this problem all you need to do is anchor every Problem-solving Question with an immediate follow-up MSA question. After the candidate finishes answering the PSQ, ask something like, "Can you now tell me about something you've actually accomplished or implemented that's most comparable to how you've suggested we handle this problem?"

Following up the Problem-solving Question by asking the person to describe a comparable major significant accomplishment is called an Anchor. Collectively, the MSA and PSQ are called the Anchor and Visualize questioning pattern. The order doesn't matter. What does matter is that for all of the critical performance objectives in the performance profile, you ask the candidates what they've accomplished that's most similar and how they would figure out and solve the problem if they were to get the job.

You will encounter some people who have difficulty with the visualization question, but have a track record of comparable past performance. The inability to figure out a solution, or even how to start, could be an indicator of nervousness, or lack of ability to see alternate options. In the latter case, the person might only be successful in very similar circumstances, cultures, and environments, so raise the caution flag.

The ability to visualize a problem and offer alternative solutions in combination with a track record of successful comparable past performance is a strong predictor of on-the-job success. One without the other is a sure path for making a bad hiring decision.

Making the Assessment Using the 1-5 Evidence-based Ranking Scale

There are some caveats to follow as you assess candidates using the general formula for hiring success. For one thing, don't make any yes/no decision until the end of the interview. Most people are overly affected by the person's first impression, good or bad, so it's best to temper this by waiting until the end of the interview to determine the candidate's suitability for the job. While it's okay to determine whether the person's first impression will impact job performance, do this at the end, when you're not personally affected by it. Review the guidelines for managing Moment 1 for more on how to get past the impact of first impression bias.

CANDIDATE ADVICE
Managing 1st Impression Bias and Moment 1

There's a lot of information in this book on how to overcome weak presentation skills, whether they're self-induced (like nervousness) or not. None of these are acceptable excuses for not being successful during the interview. However, if you don't have the "instant look," you'll need to be more persistent and do some extra things to prove that you're a person committed to be successful. On the job it means you work harder, don't make excuses, and hit your goals consistently year in and year out. It also means you're constantly improving yourself by taking extra courses, reading more books, and volunteering for the toughest assignment no one else wants. Not everyone does this. If you're this type of person, you must demonstrate this during the interview. For one thing, don't let the interviewer off the hook until the person knows what you're capable of doing. Getting past the first 30 minutes is important for everyone, whichever side of the desk you're on. There's more on this topic throughout this book, and in the chapter devoted exclusively to candidates and prospects. Advice to all candidates: read it and own it. You'll thank me later.

Another way to make sure the assessment is as objective as possible is for the interviewing team to go through each of the factors in the hiring formula together, getting specific and factual evidence from each interviewer. Using the following 1-5 ranking scale can help minimize errors caused by first impressions, over-reliance on intuition, or biases. Equally important, it will increase assessment accuracy including how different candidates for the same job are compared. The definitions provide specific guidance for each of the rankings, but it's essential that each interviewer provide comparable evidence to justify their ranking, not feelings or emotions.

Level 1: Not hirable. Not fully competent, missing a critical skill, or not motivated to do the work required under the organizational and cultural circumstances of the job. These are the people that sometimes get hired because they're good presenters or make great first impressions, but wind up in the bottom-half at performance review time.

Level 2: Competent, but not motivated to do the work required, or doesn't fit with the manager's style or company culture. Technically a fit, but not motivated to do the actual work required. Alternatively, the person doesn't have a track record of performance doing similar work recently in a similar environment, or there is a mismatch between the manager's and candidate's styles. These people are frequently very good people, put in the wrong job or situation. Hiring people like this is a very, very common hiring mistake. It's due to focusing too much on technical skills and not enough on motivation to do the work, and not assessing the situational fit factors correctly. These people ultimately fall below average when assessed against their peer group.

Level 2.5: Average performance. The person meets the basic needs of the job on all factors, including cultural and managerial fit, but the person is not exceptional in any way. While not a bad hire, the person will get the job done adequately with normal training, coaching, and supervision. The person doesn't cause problems and is easy enough to manage, but the person gets by doing reasonably good work on a consistent basis. You can also consider someone who is strong in a few areas, but weak in some others as meeting the Level 2.5 ranking.

Level 3.0: Hirable, rock-solid performance. This is a person who can achieve all of the performance objectives listed in the performance profile, and in addition, is highly motivated to do the work required. Motivation to do the work is what separates a Level 3.0 person from a Level 2.0-2.5. In addition, all measures of managerial and cultural fit are right on. This person is promotable and can take on bigger projects quickly. This person is an Achiever and is clearly in the top quartile – the top half of the top half. Performance objectives in the performance profile should be designed to fit the definition of a Level 3 person. This person is significantly above average, on a letter basis it's B+ or better.

Level 4.0: Far exceeds performance expectations. Aside from meshing on all areas of fit, this person will do more, faster, and/or better. While the person will likely exceed the performance standards of the job, the person must also be given the freedom and opportunity to perform at this higher level. To be ranked a Level 4 on an evidence basis, you'd want to see some significant recognition for the work performed. This could be in the form of a company award, being asked to coach or train a team of co-workers, or to participate in a special project based on outstanding performance.

Level 5.0: High-potential all-star. This person will achieve a level of performance far in excess of what's described in the performance profile. This is the unexpected positive surprise. It could be figuring out some remarkable new approach to accomplish something. Level 5 is more than being 15-25% better; it's about hitting it out of the park – a real game changer. There needs to be tangible evidence of recognition proving a Level 5 ranking. This is generally beyond the department, certainly at the company or industry level. Receiving a significant award from the CEO, giving a talk at an industry symposium, or being offered advanced prestigious training would be good examples of Level 5 recognition. If you find and hire a Level 5 person, the company and hiring manager must support and encourage this pushing-the-envelope behavior, otherwise dissatisfaction will quickly follow.

Group debriefing using this 1-5 evidence-based ranking approach and the formal talent scorecard included in the next chapter is an effective means for overcoming Moment 1 induced errors. Practically speaking this is as important a part of the Performance-based Interview process as everything else described in this book. Waiting 30 minutes, while sound in theory and simple to say, is hard to implement in practice, since we're preprogrammed to make instant judgments based on first impressions. However, a formal system based on commonsense rules that everyone follows can increase objectivity and minimize hiring errors caused by instant judgments and superficial assessments. "No 2s!" is one of these rules.

No 2s!

The No 2s! rule: never ever hire someone who is not highly motivated to do the work you want done.

Consider this point: the really big difference between Levels 2 and 3 and 4 is the level of motivation the person brings to the job. This is M^2 in the hiring formula. It also takes a lot of work to discern the differences between the three levels during the interview. As a result, most interviewers want to take shortcuts to get at this. Some interviewers measure it by how prepared the candidate is or how assertive. The problem is that unprepared candidates can be more hard-working once on the job, and prepared candidates less so. So this is a flawed indicator. Quiet people are no more or less motivated than outgoing people, so this is an equally flawed measure.

In too many cases, technical interviewers emphasize brilliance when the job itself requires something far less or more complete design work than system architecture. Once a person is above a technical threshold, the big differences in terms of performance are typically work-ethic, organizational and project management skills, motivation to do the actual work required, and working with all types of different people on team projects. We've all met people who are extremely competent, but not top performers, or who lack motivation to do the job. Maybe they don't like the work, the project itself, or the person is uncomfortable with the manager's style. Regardless of the cause, lack of motivation to do the actual work in the actual environment should be a deal-breaker. Motivation to do the work is the tipping point between Level 2 and Level 3 performance. Level 4 takes Level 3 motivation – which is already substantial – up a notch doing more, doing it better, or doing it faster.

Hiring a Level 3 or Level 4 person is never a problem; they're both in the top quartile. In fact, frequently a Level 3 person can become a Level 4 depending on the work assignment, and vice-versa. Level 2s are another matter entirely. Following the "No 2s!" rule can minimize the number one hiring error of all time: hiring people who make good impressions, are competent to do the work, but require extra management and pushing to achieve average results. If you want to hire self-motivated and self-directed people, make sure you don't break the "No 2s!" rule.

To ensure "No 2s!" interviewers need to get detailed examples as part of every MSA question where the candidate took the initiative, went above the call of duty, volunteered for something, or ensured the work got done without making excuses. If you seek this out as part of the fact-finding you'll see a pattern emerge of the types of work that highly motivates the candidate to excel. For some it will cover a broad range of activities, for others it will be highly specific tasks, and for others very little motivates them. To ensure someone is a Level 3 or 4, and not a Level 2 for the job at hand, you need to find recent examples of drive and motivation doing the work described in the performance profile.

Having done similar work fairly recently is an important part of the performance-based assessment. This is common with people who might be considered over-qualified. There are many people who might have once been highly motivated to do the work required, but no longer find the work of interest. They're competent, but unmotivated. Yet these historic examples are used to demonstrate their current prowess and motivation. Raise the caution flag if the person hasn't shown this high level of motivation in the past few years. If this is the case, the motivation might be short-lived.

*C**AUTION: Do not accept even the most vocal or sincere statement from any candidate that he/she will do the work required without complete proof of recent past performance.***

Often pre-hire statements of willingness to do anything required are driven by economic need. Once this need is met, motivation will only be driven by a higher-order need, typically sincere interest in the work.

On the other hand, if the person has demonstrated a high degree of self-motivation in whatever type of work assigned or set of work circumstances, seriously consider the person. This is a person of high character and commitment. Some of this evidence could be taking advanced training, continual self-development in the area of interest, or a "do whatever it takes" attitude.

Following "No 2s!" in combination with the "Wait 30 Minutes!" rule will go a long way towards increasing assessment accuracy. Putting your emotions in the parking lot is comparable to a judge requiring the jury to listen to all of the evidence before reaching a verdict. You'll discover that by waiting 30 minutes you'll be able to assign the candidates into one of three big categories: those that are either Level 1s or Level 5s, or somewhere in-between. Unfortunately, somewhere in-between is a big gap and the differences between a person who is competent and unmotivated and competent and highly motivated are very subtle. By having "No 2s!" drive your fact-finding, seeking details and specific facts, you'll be able to see the differences and confidently rank your candidate a Level 2, 3, or 4. This is what you'll do after waiting 30 minutes.

But making this assessment is not possible without a performance profile. The evidence you're seeking is not generic motivation, but motivation to handle the tasks and projects defined in the performance profile. When these two rules are combined with the 1-5 scale ranking of each factor in the hiring formula, you'll be able to eliminate most hiring mistakes caused by omission, emotion, intuition, or technical overkill.

CANDIDATE ADVICE
Handling the Over-qualified Concern

....

Consider Maslow's Hierarchy of Needs (budurl.com/agmas1) as you evaluate your personal job-hunting situation. Abraham Maslow was a mid-20th century psychologist who studied the behavior of high-performing individuals. In a 1943 paper, he suggested that people make fundamental and predictable decisions based on different behavioral needs. These needs range from primitive low-order needs, like requiring water or food, to higher-order needs like achievement and recognition. He separated these states into five distinct levels and referred to them collectively as a hierarchy of needs. According to Maslow, a person couldn't move to a higher level unless the needs of the lower level were satisfied first. The graphic summarizes this hierarchy in the form of a pyramid.

According to Maslow, and common sense, your job-hunting activity and related decision-making will all be affected by whether you're fully employed and highly satisfied, or underemployed, or not employed at all. Even if you're in a job you thoroughly enjoy, you might entertain the possibility of something better, which is driven by the achievement need. If you're unemployed or underemployed, economic and security needs will drive your motivation and decision-making. In this latter state, you might be forced to take a job below your capabilities and be more than willing to do it. You'll even state this publicly and actually believe it. After all, it's true. But only temporarily.

According to Maslow, and again common sense, once this lower-order economic need is satisfied your satisfaction with the job itself will naturally decline. As a result your work performance will suffer and you'll seek other job opportunities that meet a higher-order need. This is why employers are reluctant to hire people who appear "overqualified." I agree. My advice to employers is to only hire people who are highly motivated to do the actual work required. If a person appears over-qualified, I would only recommend hiring the person if he/she has done similar work in the recent past at a high level of performance. For example, a person who has been an engineering manager, but still does exceptional detailed design work and finds it extremely satisfying should be seriously considered. The caveat though is that the person has demonstrated this level of performance recently. This could be in the form of self-development activity or recent work experience.

I remember speaking with a PhD in Chemical Engineering a number of years ago who complained he was considered over-qualified even though he could do the work and was exceptional at it. I then asked him when he last did this type of work. He told me it was over 10 years ago, with the tag, "But it doesn't matter."

But it does! This person was way beyond doing this type of work. He'd only do it while the economic need existed. If you're a candidate faced with similar employer concerns about your "over-qualifications," you can do a couple of things to address the problem:

Prove you always work at peak levels regardless of the task at hand. Some people are blessed with an extraordinary work-ethic, commitment, and level of responsibility. If you can demonstrate with real examples that you're one of these rare people, an employer would be foolish in dismissing you out-of-hand. Multiple examples of proof are required, though, and they need to be recent, substantive, and relevant. In essence you must demonstrate via actual recent accomplishments examples of doing work below your current professional level and doing it extremely well.

Demonstrate that you've done similar types of work recently in the past at high levels of quality. This is a lesser burden of proof than the idea above, but it's still imposing. In this case you just need to demonstrate, again with actual examples of recent work, that the type of work the company requires for on-the-job success is work that both motivates you, and is work you're good at. The work doesn't need to be identical, though, just comparable. One way to better understand this is to ask the interviewer to describe the work required in some detail and how performance will be measured. For a managerial position it could be building, coaching, and training a team to implement a specific process or procedure. For a technical position it could be pulling a spec together or designing a specific project.

During this questioning you need to think about some recent accomplishment that best demonstrates your ability. Then as one comes to mind, make sure you describe this accomplishment in detail and give the dates and duration. For example, if the interviewer doesn't mention working on a cross-functional team or being responsible for budgeting and planning, ask if these things are important. If they are, describe some recent accomplishment that covers this. This type of force-the-question is a great way to get the interviewer to ask you about your strengths. As a result, don't be surprised that the job gets adjusted or expanded to meet your level. Asking direct, job-related questions like this is viewed positively by most hiring managers, primarily since only people who have a great deal of self-confidence would ask them.

Bargain for some relief. Use the same force-the-question technique described above to find out the complete scope of the job. While some components of the job might be less desirable than others, the total mix might be acceptable. If the company thinks you're a strong person they actually might modify the job a bit to better meet your needs, but you need to ask them if this is a possibility. You'll never get to this point unless you are fully prepared (as described later in this book) and you're self-confident enough to ask the interviewer to describe the real job requirements. You should do this anyway, even if you're not carrying the "over-qualified" mantle, since no one should accept a job unless they know exactly what's expected of them. Being surprised about what you'll be doing after you've accepted an offer is a recipe for disappointment.

Take a short-term temp or consulting position. Rather than asking the company to take the risk of you becoming dissatisfied due to being overqualified, suggest that you'll be willing to prove both your competence and motivation on a trial basis. This could be in the form of a short-term gig or doing some type of consulting project. This allows the company to see your capabilities in action and if you "fit" their culture. You then have a chance to determine whether the job fits your needs.

....

Summary – The Two-Question Performance-based Interview

- **The Most Significant Accomplishment Question (MSA).** It's important to ask the candidate to describe a specific accomplishment for each objective listed in the performance profile. Most candidates won't do this naturally or provide too much detail. To counter this, the interviewer needs to take responsibility for getting this information by peeling the onion and detailed fact-finding. This is the only way to get a complete understanding of what the candidate actually accomplished and under what circumstances. The trend line of these accomplishments over time is very revealing – whether they're up, down, or going sideways.

- **The Problem-solving Question (PSQ).** It's important to assess thinking and problem-solving skills in relation to real job needs, but you can't do this by asking hypothetical or trick questions. Instead, ask candidates how they'd solve real, job-related problems. By getting into a give-and-take dialogue around this problem, the interviewer can assess how the person would solve the problem. This approach measures the person's ability to develop the process and implement the solution, not the solution itself.

- **The Anchor and Visualize Pattern.** Sometimes candidates can tell you how they would solve a problem, but aren't actually able to implement what they say they'd do. To assess this, after answering a Problem-solving Question, ask the candidate to describe something he or she has accomplished that's most comparable. This is called an Anchor to the PSQ visualization question. This ensures the person can walk the talk. Candidates who are great with the PSQ visualization question, but have weak MSA anchors, typically are better at planning and problem-solving than execution. Those who have strong accomplishments, but are weaker on the problem-solving side, tend to be more structured in their thinking and less flexible.

- **The 1-5 Ranking Scale.** The ranking system suggested is not linear. On this scale a 2.5 is representative of the average person working at your company in a comparable job. Levels 3-5 are all remarkable people and hirable, representative of the top 25% of your current workforce. Level 4s do more than what's described on the performance profile, or do it better or do it faster. Level 5s take their work to another level entirely. It's actually relatively easy to figure out who's a Level 1 or Level 5 using most reasonable interviewing techniques. Unfortunately, Levels 2, 3, and 4 can all look pretty much alike using these same techniques. Waiting 30 minutes and the "No 2s!" rules can help sort out these differences.

- **No 2s!** Preventing hiring mistakes is actually more important than hiring super-stars. In the long run, hiring people who are competent, but unmotivated to do the work required, impacts everyone negatively, especially the hiring manager. This is a very common hiring mistake caused by lack of job knowledge, lack of objectively, and the use of superficial interviewing techniques. The idea behind No 2s! is to use the interview to focus on the candidate's motivation, drive, and initiative doing work similar to what's described in the performance profile. This is only possible if the interviewer knows these actual job requirements and can conduct an in-depth objective interview. No 2s! means you'll only be hiring Levels 3, 4, and 5 – all great people and great hires.

- **Candidates: Handling the Over-qualified Concern.** Having the ability to do something is much different than having the will or motivation to do it. Rather than complaining after the fact that you didn't get the job because you were deemed over-qualified, use the interview to prove you are both competent and motivated to do the work needed. To do this, first make sure you ask about the actual work required. Then you must give proof of having done similar work recently and at high quality. As part of this provide specific examples of going the extra mile, pushing through challenges, and taking the initiative. Recent and comparable are the keys to success.

Chapter 5

Organizing the Interview and Making the Assessment

U sing the two-question performance-based interview in combination with the hiring formula for success is a great way to assess competency, motivation, and organizational fit. However, it can't, or shouldn't, be done alone.

The hiring team must get together before the final decision is made and share what they've learned. This requires that some type of formal debriefing be part of the assessment as well as some up-front organization and planning. The key is to assign specific roles to everyone on the interviewing team, where everyone shares their evidence for each of the factors. One way to do this is to assign each interviewer a few of the factors in the hiring formula for success. By preventing anyone from having a full yes/no vote you increase the need for every interviewer to be more responsible and objective. In this approach the hiring team makes the yes/no decision. This collective type of focused interview in combination with a formal debriefing is a great way to minimize the impact of emotions, biases, feelings, and weak interviewing skills during the final evaluation.

Using the 1-5 ranking scale can also help minimize the impact of feelings and emotions. Under no circumstances should you allow the interviewing team to add up individual yes/no votes to make this decision. In most debriefing sessions the hiring team gets together and shares their opinions in some informal way. The range of these rankings varies across the board, with those with more authority having more influence. Most likely these people also conducted shorter interviews, just to see if the person "fits." These short interviews are useless and should be banned! There's not enough time in 30 minutes to determine anything substantive. Reviewing all of the factors in the hiring formula as a team using the 1-5 ranking scale is how the debriefing should be conducted.

Our complete Quality of Hire Talent Scorecard is shown here. There is another copy in the Appendix (and purchasers of this book can download a PDF version). You'll notice it maps directly to the hiring formula. I suggest using this form to guide the debriefing session with each member of the interviewing team being assigned a few of the factors to "own."

THE QUALITY OF HIRE TALENT SCORECARD

Factor	Level 1 Minimal	Level 2 Adequate	Average 2.5	Level 3 Strong	Level 4 Great	Level 5 Superb	
BASIC FIT							
Skills	Bare minimum.	Has the basics, but needs help.	Covers all direct job needs well.	Extremely strong in all job needs.	Brings far more to table.		>8
Experience	Minimum threshold.	Meets most, but not all needs.	Meets all experience needs.	Broader experience.	Perfect fit plus more.		
Achiever Pattern	No evidence the person is in the top 50%.	Some, but not sure if person is in top 50%.	Evidence clearly indicates person is top 25%!	Evidence clearly indicates person is in top 10-15%.	Evidence clearly indicates person is in top 5%.		
CORE COMPETENCIES							
Talent & Technical	Meets bare minimum standards. Needs too much support.	Can do the work, but needs added training, support.	Technically tops. An asset. Can learn quickly. Covers it all.	Top-notch. Trains others. Constantly improving. Brings more to the table.	Brilliant. Sets standards. Leader in field. Sought out. Recognized.		>10
Management	Unorganized. Very reactive. Misses most deadlines.	Needs direction, monitoring. More reactive than plan.	Solid planner, organizer. Executes well. Anticipates issues.	Excellent. Plans, anticipates, communicates, and succeeds.	Handles complex projects. Makes it happen. Anticipates everything.		
Team	Little team growth. Limited examples of leading or influencing others.	Some team growth, but needs urging. Okay examples of influencing others.	Good team growth. Has taken on bigger team roles.	Clear team track. Takes initiative to help others. Takes lead.	Impressive team growth. Persuades, motivates, coaches. Asked to lead.		
Thinking & Problem-solving	Didn't understand any key issues or develop any solutions.	Understood most issues, developed okay solutions.	Clearly understood all key issues and developed very well.	Understood all key & less obvious issues. Works w/ others. Developed multiple solutions.	Seeks best solutions. Understood core issues & provides new insights.		
SITUATIONAL FIT FACTORS							
Job Fit	Limited comparability with accomplishments and job needs.	Some comparable accomplishments, but limited or inconsistent.	Accomplishments clearly comparable with consistent results.	Achieved better results doing similar work in similar environments.	Full job match with exceptional results – scope, pace, resources.		>10
Managerial Fit	Mismatch between candidate's & manager's style.	Limited, but has worked with similar managers.	Successfully worked with similar managers.	Person easily adapts to a variety of manager styles.	Super fit. Coaches upward. Both are flexible.		
Culture & Environment	Complete mismatch on culture & environment.	Reasonable match on culture and environment.	Close match on culture and environment.	Excellent match and has made similar transfers.	Thrives in this type of environment, culture.		
Motivation[2]	Very limited evidence of motivation to do this type of work.	Will do the core work, but needs extra pushing.	Self-motivated to do this type of work w/ normal supervision.	Takes initiative to do more, faster, & better. Self-improves in this type of work.	Totally committed to do whatever it takes to get it done. Constant self-development.		

The Quality of Hire Talent Scorecard Maps Directly to the Hiring Formula and the Full Performance-based Interview

Although each interviewer will ask the same core accomplishment and Problem-solving Questions, their focus will be on their assigned factors. The idea here is to ask more in-depth fact-finding questions to fully understand how a specific factor was used to accomplish the major task. For example, for the person assigned the "Team" factor, he/she would make sure enough follow-up questions were asked to understand the person's team role and impact.

Some typical team-based follow-up questions are: who was on the team, what was your exact role, please describe the biggest team challenge, how did you influence the team, and how did the team influence you. (Later in this chapter you'll find a full list of team-related fact-finding questions.)

It's also okay to modify the main MSA question to address any of the factors in the hiring formula. For example, the interviewer could ask the person to describe his/her most significant technical or management accomplishment. The majority of the subsequent fact-finding would then be asked to fully understand the primary competency or trait factor being assessed.

Using the Quality of Hire Talent Scorecard

As you review this section make sure you review the full Performance-based Interview and Quality of Hire Talent Scorecard. It's important to fully understand how to use the Quality of Hire Talent Scorecard form. The Hiring Formula for Success factors are shown in the first column with specific guidance for the 1-5 rankings for each factor shown in the adjacent columns. The form is divided into three sections to follow the method suggested using the structured Performance-based Interview. The idea is to first assess general fit, and if the person passes this hurdle, expand the assessment to address the core competencies and then the situational fit factors. Following the "No 2s!" rule, the person would need to achieve a score of at least an "8" on the Basic Fit factors to move ahead and at least a total of "10" on both the Core and Situational Fit factors to be considered a serious candidate.

The three Basic Fit factors (i.e., Skills, Experience, and Achiever Pattern) can be used to help guide the tradeoff between skills and experience, and potential, with the Achiever Pattern representing potential. The idea behind this is to seriously consider someone who might be a little light either on the skills or experience side, but strong on potential. Note that the use of a performance profile defining Level 3 performance allows the hiring manager to convert skills and experience into a realistic performance objective. This allows for a much more meaningful assessment of ability rather than relying on some arbitrary and absolute level (e.g., "Must have 3-5 years of experience").

First determine whether the person has enough skills and experience to do the work as defined in the performance profile at a high level of performance. If not, the second determination is figuring out if the person has enough upside potential to lessen some of the job requirements. For this trade-off to be successful, the manager or someone else needs to be in a position to coach or train the person. In addition, the business situation has to allow time for the new hire to learn. I'd suggest a total score of at least an "8" on this first section before moving on to a more in-depth interview. I'd also suggest being a little liberal on the ranking. If a person is close, it's certainly appropriate to ask additional questions about the person's core competencies to see if you missed something. Of course, if the person ranks no more than a Level 2 on each of the three factors, diplomatically end the interview, or recommend the person for a different role. (Reminder Note: all of the ranking is in relationship to the actual job opening. As a result someone can be Level 2 for one job and a Level 5 for another.)

Understanding the 1-5 Ranking Scale

Keep in mind that a Level 3 is a desirable and hirable person, so achieving this level is remarkable. It represents a person who can do the required work described in the performance profile very well and, as a result, is promotable.

Many people get somewhat upset when I say this, contending they only want to hire 5s. This is more aspirational than actually possible, or desirable. It's impossible for one thing, since in the 1-5 ranking definition there are too few of them to go around. Worse, it would result in chaos.

*H*aving all MVPs on the team makes it
destined to fail. I suggest a mix of 3s, 4s,
and 5s is an ideal group make-up. Everyone's
a first-teamer this way, a few are all-stars, and
an MVP will show up every now and then.

Getting the ranking right is not as simple as it sounds, and requires
some diligence. During the formal debriefing the idea is to discuss
specific examples of performance to make an assessment for any of
the factors. For example using the "Team" factor, a person would
need to have shown growth in the types of teams the person has been
assigned to or led to achieve a Level 3 ranking. In this case, concluding
the person is a Level 3 because he/she seems friendly or warm is not
sufficient to assign a team skills ranking. On the other hand, a Level 3
ranking would be appropriate for someone who is quiet, but has been
assigned to, or asked to join, larger multi-functional teams in most of
their recent past jobs. The talent scorecard will help guide the depth of
evidence required to make the assessment. Emotions and feelings are
not appropriate for making any judgment, good or bad.

It's important for the group to put special focus on motivation, and
judge this without compromise. This is the "No 2s!" rule. Motivation
is the core driver of success, and it's much more than being assertive in
the interview or being well-prepared. In the hiring formula it's squared
to emphasize its importance. Most important, to accurately assess it,
it also must be judged relative to the below-the-line fit factors in the
hiring formula: job fit, managerial fit, and cultural fit. Motivation can't
be judged properly without this conditional relationship.

The earlier Maslow discussion can help you understand the source of
motivation. If a person has an economic need to take a job, motivation might be short-lived, unless the underlying work is intrinsically
satisfying. During the assessment it's important to ask the person why
they're looking for a job and what they're looking for in a new job. Ask
how the person will make the decision if they receive multiple offers
and how they'll prioritize the factors in order of importance. This will

give you some sense of what is currently motivating the candidate's job-hunting efforts. Bottom line, though, if the person hasn't demonstrated recent enthusiasm for the type of work your job entails, or hasn't taken the initiative doing the actual work required in the recent past, raise the caution flag.

Determining Whether the Interview Process is Loosey-Goosey

The interview process at most companies is more free-ranging than controlled, with each manager doing his/her own thing. This is typically wrapped in a debriefing process that gives those who vote no and those in authority more power than a yes based on insight, judgment, and evidence. You can gain a quick sense of how meaningful and in-control your company's interviewing process is by examining the range of variances among the interviewers for each factor that's being deliberated. Wide differences are indicative of weak, out-of-control processes.

This problem has been addressed using the talent scorecard and the 1-5 ranking system. When real evidence is shared in a group setting, the range of difference should be within plus or minus a half a point. Any more than this is a sign someone on the interviewing team is measuring the candidate either superficially or using a biased approach. For example, if someone is really a Level 3, the interviewing team rankings would range from 2.5 to 3.5. If the rankings range from 2.0 to 4.0, you can conclude the collective interviewing process is flawed. As you'll discover, sharing more real, unbiased evidence will naturally tighten the range of differences among members of the interviewing team.

From a loss prevention standpoint, hiring success is less about hiring more Level 4s and 5s, and more about not hiring Level 2s. This is why following the "No 2s!" rule is so important. In some cases, you might want to hire a high-potential but lighter person who is a Level 2.0-2.5 on current skills or some less critical factor, but who can learn quickly. In general I would suggest being very cautious when violating the "No 2s!" rule. The big point: you will never be surprised about a short-coming following the "No 2s!" rule. The following table will help you understand what you need to know to prevent hiring a Level 2 for the factors shown on the scorecard.

The No 2s! Guidance Table

Factor	The Caution Flags
Motivation[2]	No pattern of taking initiative in critical needs areas. Hard to pull out examples of going the extra mile. Inconsistent.
Talent	No evidence of person doing exceptional work, influencing others on technical matters, or understanding how to solve basic tech problems.
Management	Makes excuses for tasks not being met. Does not have a track record of consistently committing and delivering. Planning is haphazard.
Team	Lack of 360° growth, no evidence of coaching others, or being asked to participate or lead a team project.
Thinking	Lack of clarity around problem-solving approach and little evidence of handling similar issues successfully.
Job Fit	Competent, but few examples of being truly motivated to do the majority of the actual work required.
Manager Fit	Hasn't excelled under a variety of different managers, or where did excel, style was different than new hiring manager.
Culture, Environment	Person's best work was different from pace, resources, decision-making process than company culture.

Hiring Great People Starts By Avoiding Obvious Mistakes.

The Performance-based Interview involves having a candidate provide relevant examples of accomplishments that are most comparable to those listed in the performance profile. It often takes 15 minutes (sometimes longer) to fully understand each accomplishment and the candidate's actual role. By sharing the results of these accomplishments in a formal debriefing session using the Quality of Hire Talent Scorecard as a guide, the ability to predict a candidate's on-the-job performance is greatly enhanced. The key to success in using this form is the mutual sharing of evidence (i.e., specific facts, dates, and details) to support the ranking, rather than adding up a bunch of yes/no votes, or basing the assessment on feelings, emotions, or biases.

In the final analysis, avoiding Level 2 performance is more important than figuring out if the person is a 3, 4, or 5. Level 2s, while competent, are not fully motivated to handle all aspects of the job, requiring more management direction and demotivating their co-workers who have to pick up the slack. Level 3s and above are all fully competent to handle the requirements of the job, and are all good hires. Some might be able to handle more work, do it faster, or produce better quality, but this is in large part due to circumstances, not just natural ability. Bottom line: follow the "No 2s!" rule and you won't go wrong.

Organizing the Interview and Debriefing Session

The idea behind the Performance-based Hiring process is pretty simple. Prepare a performance profile for the job, look for basic fit and the Achiever Pattern, ask the two core questions, and use the Hiring Formula and the Quality of Hire Scorecard to make the assessment. However, the question most people ask is, "Does everyone ask the same questions?" The answer is yes, but not exactly.

TEAM FACT-FINDING PROBES

- Who was on the team?
- What was your role?
- How did you get assigned to the team?
- What were the team's objectives?
- How did you help accomplish these?
- Who did you influence?
- Who influenced you?
- Who coached you?
- Who did you coach?
- What was the biggest team failure?
- Did you get any formal recognition from the team?
- How could your team role have been better?
- How did you deal with conflict?
- How did you grow as a team player?

Start by assigning each interviewer a subset of the factors in the hiring formula to focus on using the same two questions. This is better than giving everyone a full yes/no vote. For example, if someone is assigned team skills to "own," the interviewer would find examples of the candidate's biggest team-related accomplishments and fact-find around these. Some typical team probes are shown above. Asking an MSA question and using the team-based fact-finding will give the interviewer great insight around this factor. During the debriefing session this person would present their findings and then defend their 1-5 ranking with evidence. Everyone else could then chime in, and provide either supporting or contradictory evidence.

It's very difficult for one person to assess all of the factors effectively, so divvying them up makes good sense. The table that follows can be used to assign roles to each member of the interviewing team. Overlapping the factors is certainly fine and recommended.

The idea of having each interviewer focus on a narrower and different subset of factors allows for the whole team to be involved in the process. Assessments are much more accurate when someone is responsible for just a few of the factors, since the evidence is much richer than having everyone assess everything. This is also much better than adding up biased yes/no votes. The concept of yes/no voting should be banned anyway, since this alone assumes everyone knows how to conduct a full and effective objective interview, which is rare. Worse, it rewards the superficial interviewer, since it's much safer to vote no rather than yes. If you've ever been involved in these debriefing sessions, it's pretty obvious that "no" becomes the default vote when people are asked to defend their position. No one wants to be told "I told you so," after the person starts and underperforms, so voting no is easier and more comfortable. Another issue with a yes/no voting system: the highest-ranking person in the room can usually sway everyone else to his/her way of thinking, unfounded or not. It's hard to argue with the boss. Sharing evidence for each of the factors in the hiring formula prevents many of these problems.

Use the table to assign each person on the interviewing team a group of factors (2-4 is appropriate) to focus on during the interview. No interview should be less than 45 minutes either, since you can't really obtain any substantive information in less time. In most cases, the first 15 minutes are wasted by the impact of first impressions. For this type of secondary or targeted interview, I'd give each interviewer on the team at least one of the core factors to own and one situational fit factor. Even though their focus is narrower using this approach, each interviewer will be able to provide some insight on the other factors during the debriefing session. This is only natural since there's so much information exchanged using the two-question methodology. Regardless, you'll discover each of the interviewer's insights will be greater by narrowing their focus, as suggested.

ORGANIZE THE INTERVIEW TO MAXIMUM ASSESSMENT ACCURACY

Factor	Recruiter HR	Hiring Manager	One	Two	Three
Skills					
Experience					
Achiever Pattern					
CORE COMPETENCIES					
Talent & Technical					
Management					
Team					
Thinking, Problem-solving					
SITUATIONAL FIT FACTORS					
Job Fit					
Managerial Fit					
Culture					
Motivation[2]					

Assign Each Interviewer 2-3 of the Factors in the Hiring Formula to "Own"

During the debriefing, use the talent scorecard to guide the assessment, asking for evidence for each of the factors, one by one. Don't start with a yes/no vote or "How do you feel?" process. This will be obvious by the end of the debriefing session. Remember that a wide swing, around any of the factors, indicates more work is necessary before an accurate assessment can be made. A variation of plus or minus .5 points is pretty typical if all of the interviewers have conducted objective assessments, and everyone has heard all of the evidence. Most people will alter their viewpoint in the face of real evidence, so this full sharing is a critical piece of the assessment process.

CANDIDATE ADVICE
How to Ace the Interview

Make sure you reverse engineer yourself by reading this chapter at least a dozen times. There's a dual purpose in this. First, become great at interviewing others. Then when you're the candidate, you'll know exactly what to do. The key to all of this is that when you're a candidate interviewing for a job, you need to make sure you can present yourself as someone who is both competent and motivated to do the work required. Here are some specific things you can do to make sure you get this "competent and motivated" point across:

- Early in the interview, ask the interviewer to describe the actual job and big challenges involved. You'll be answering these questions by providing examples of your most relevant accomplishments.

- As the interviewer describes the job, find out what the big performance objectives for the position are. For example, "What's the biggest problem that you need solved?" Review the section on preparing performance profiles to help guide this questioning. Your job is to create a mini performance profile real time during the interview. This is important, since most hiring managers won't have done this, and you'll get points for being direct and insightful.

- Ask related questions as you're finding out about real job needs. Find out why the position is open, what resources are available, how performance will be measured, the big challenges, and the timeline.

- Once you understand what the most important performance objectives are for the job, provide your best examples of where you've done similar work at high levels of performance. Make sure you answer this question with specific details as described in the section on getting ready for the interview and preparing for Moment 1.

- At the end of the interview state your interest in learning more, summarize what you've heard, state your concerns (you must have them) and some questions you'd like answered in the next round if you're invited back, and ask about the next steps. Don't be too eager. The quality of your questions in combination with a general statement of interest is more than sufficient.

- If the interviewer is non-committal, push a little with respect to timing. If this doesn't work, ask the interviewer if, based on what he/she knows about you, the person would recommend you for the next step. If not, find out why, and try to give an example of something that would increase the interviewer's confidence that you're someone the company should seriously consider.

None of this will work if you don't cite specific examples of actual relevant accomplishments. So don't skip a single step!

··

Summary – Organizing the Interview and Making the Assessment

- **Use the Quality of Hire Talent Scorecard to make the assessment.** Assessment accuracy is increased by assessing a candidate across all measures of job performance in comparison to the requirements described in the performance profile. The scorecard follows the Performance-based Interview process I recommend, covering all of the factors in the hiring formula. Using the scorecard this way offers a means to measure pre-hire Quality of Hire. Since all of the factors are in relation to the actual job, this same scorecard can also be used to measure Quality of Hire post-hire. Any pre- and post-hire variations can then be used as feedback to improve the assessment process.

- **Understand the importance of the 1-5 ranking scale.** Specific evidence is needed before assigning a candidate a 1-5 ranking for any of the factors. These rankings are based on facts, details, and examples of actual work performance, not feelings, emotions, or guesses. Assessment accuracy is increased by having each interviewer share their evidence, justifying their ranking. Be concerned when the rankings among the interviewers vary by more than plus or minus a half point on any of the factors. This is indicative of a flawed or superficial interviewing process.

- **Look for the Achiever Pattern.** Those in the top 25% of their peer group often get external and formal recognition for their exceptional work. This is typically in the form of bigger raises, faster promotions, assignments to bigger multi-functional teams and/or more critical projects, a special award, or a unique honor. This is a strong indicator of a top person, especially when observed over time in multiple jobs and with different companies. Collectively this is the Achiever Pattern. Look for it during the early part of the phone screening process and during the full interview. If you're a candidate make sure you highlight this information in your resume, your LinkedIn profile, and during the interview.

- **Organize the interview to increase assessment accuracy.** Rather than give every interviewer a full yes/no hiring vote, it's best to assign each person a subset of the factors on the talent scorecard. Although they'll use the same two questions (MSA and PSQ) during the interview, their focus will be narrower, obtaining very specific evidence to develop an evidence-based 1-5 ranking score for the factors assigned to them. During the debriefing session go through the scorecard form from top to bottom, with each of the assigned interviewers sharing their evidence to justify their ranking.

- **Ban the 30-minute interview and the Yes/No voting system.** There is not enough time in 30 minutes to predict anything about on-the-job performance. In fact, these types of interviews force superficial assessments based on first impressions, personal biases, and over-reliance on intuition. When short interviews like this are combined with a yes/no voting system, the chance of making an accurate assessment is remote. The problem is that no votes are safer than yes votes, and as a result are used more often, especially by those who conducted superficial interviews. Yes/no voting also gives those in authority more power, since most subordinates will submit to their assessments whether they've conducted a complete interview or not.

- **Candidates – make sure you're assessed properly.** Unfortunately most interviewers will make a judgment about you on first impressions, how assertive you are, if you're friendly or not, and how well you communicate. Very little of this correlates with your ability and motivation to do the work required. You can minimize many of these problems by asking early in the interview about real job needs. Then you must give relevant and detailed examples of work you've done that's most comparable. Don't over-talk, though. Instead, give substantive answers that entice the interviewer to ask follow-up questions.

Chapter 6

Understanding Real Job Needs – The Performance Profile

Throughout this book I've mentioned the idea of using performance profiles to define the actual job as superior to relying on traditional job descriptions. I also refer to these as performance-based job descriptions. Let me be perfectly clear about my feelings on this point, if you haven't figured them out already.

From what I've seen working with hundreds of companies around the world for over 30 years, traditional job descriptions listing skills and experiences are the most useless documents ever created for hiring purposes.

For one thing, having the skills and experiences listed in the job description doesn't guarantee success. For another, they exclude high-potential people from consideration who are either high-achievers who don't need as much experience or strong people who have a different mix of skills. Worse, very few high achievers with the skills and experience listed are willing to take, or even consider, a job that appears on the surface to be nothing more than a lateral transfer.

Using performance profiles to define actual job needs eliminates all of these problems. Furthermore, as described in the General Legal Validation by David Goldstein of Littler Mendelson, they are in full legal compliance with U.S. labor laws, and, in fact, allow you to easily hire more diverse talent, including returning military veterans. A summary of his full report is included in the Appendix but here's his quick perspective on the use of performance profiles:

> *A properly prepared performance profile can identify and document the essential functions of a job better than traditional position descriptions, facilitating the reasonable accommodation of disabilities and making it easier to comply with the Americans with Disabilities Act and similar laws.*

A performance profile describes the main performance objectives a person taking the job needs to do to be successful. It differs from a job description in that it doesn't describe skills or traits, but rather what the person needs to accomplish with these skills and traits. When measuring competency, interest, and fit, it's always better to describe what the person needs to DO, rather than what the person needs to HAVE. For example, instead of saying the person must have five years of international accounting experience and a CPA, it's better to say "Integrate the SAP international reporting system by the end of Q2." Then when asking the MSA question, all that the interviewer needs to do is provide a quick summary of the objective and ask the candidate to describe an accomplishment that is most comparable. For the PSQ question, the interviewer can first describe not only the objective, but also some of the challenges and problems involved with completing the task, and then ask the candidate how he/she would go about solving the problem or achieving the task.

Of course, a person needs enough skills and experience to achieve the results defined, but this varies depending on the capability of the person. If you've determined the candidate can achieve the performance objective, it's clear he or she has exactly the right level of skills and experience needed.

How to Prepare Performance Profiles

A typical performance profile consists of three to four major objectives with the balance being the critical subtasks that need to be accomplished along the way. For example, if the major objective is implementing the SAP reporting system, a subtask might be "During the first 30 days evaluate the status of the overall project and ensure the resources are available to complete the project on time and budget."

Performance Profile Example for International Consolidations Project Leader

1) Working with IT and group accounting, take the lead on integrating the SAP international reporting system by the end of Q2.

2) During the first 30 days determine the current status of the project and prepare a detailed plan-of-action including timelines and critical deliverables.

3) Identify critical technical, system, or consolidation issues that need to be resolved to complete the project on schedule.

4) Present a formal project plan to the senior financial team for approval within 45 days identifying all critical issues and specific resource and manpower requirements.

5)   Lead the test and evaluation of the consolidations module by Q3 with special focus on the integration with budgeting and annual operating plan variance analysis.

Performance profiles like these can be created for any type of job, from entry-level to senior executive. Here's another example for a customer service rep for an inbound call center:

Performance Profile Example for Customer Service Rep

1)   Within 90 days be in a position to complete 30+ inbound calls per day from current clients handling all of the necessary updates to their company benefit programs.

2)   Pass the 30-day training program and master the user interface and dashboard reporting system. Within 60 days, be in a position to coach new users.

3)   On an ongoing basis, handle 4-5 open calls at any given time, prioritize all inbound calls by complexity, and target a closure rate of 80% at an average of seven minutes per call.

4)   Due to the high-volume, structured nature of this activity, 100% attendance is needed with frequent overtime expected.

5)   Achieve a 95% or better rating on the customer satisfaction survey reporting system.

Clarifying expectations is the driving force behind job satisfaction and performance. This is basic management 101, but in the rush to fill positions this principle is somehow ignored, overlooked, or forgotten. Spending an extra 30 minutes upfront to prepare a performance profile is a lot easier and time-friendly than hiring someone who needs constant pushing to achieve average performance. These are the Level 2 hires mentioned in previous chapters. While motivation is the most important driver of on-the-job success, it must be measured in comparison to real job needs. A performance profile captures all of this: job fit, managerial fit, and cultural fit.

While the above examples of performance profiles are okay for getting started, more information is usually required to fully understand real job needs. The SMARTe acronym introduced earlier as part of the questioning process can also help prepare and clarify the performance objectives. The idea: clarify the objective by making it **S**pecific, **M**easurable, **A**ction-oriented, include the **R**esult, the **T**ime frame, and an overriding statement about the **e**nvironment. The environment relates to the culture, management issues, resource availability, or unique challenges involved in completing the task successfully. A complete SMARTe objective for the major SAP project might look something like this:

> *Along with the IS and internal audit departments, take the project lead role for fully integrating the SAP international reporting system by the end of Q2. This project is currently three months behind schedule and a new project plan, additional resources, and an increased focus is necessary to meet the project plan requirements.*

Following are the basic steps involved in figuring out the critical performance objectives for most types of jobs:

First, define the 3-4 major performance objectives. These are the things you'd tell a candidate they would be expected to accomplish during the first 3-12 months on the job. Don't even look at the job description to figure these out. Just write down the big things the new hire will be working on. For a software developer these could be tasks like design a new user interface, find out why the system crashes all the time, and work with marketing to prepare a new product requirements document. Then put the tasks in priority order, and make the most important ones as SMARTe as possible, including some measure of performance and a timeframe.

Convert HAVING to DOING. Now you can look at the job description. Review the skills and experience requirements listed and see if they're covered in the major objectives list above. If not, describe some task the person will actually be doing on the job that requires this skill. This can be pretty basic, just an action verb and a basic description will suffice. For a plant engineer requiring 5-8 years of robotics maintenance background, the task might be "Implement a process improvement program with the goal of reducing downtime by 50%." These should then be added to the master list of major performance objectives, prioritized along with the others and made as SMARTe as possible.

Next, break the major objectives into sub-tasks. The process of achieving a major accomplishment always requires the successful completion of a sequenced series of sub-tasks. For sales it's finding leads and making presentations, for engineering it could be figuring out the design problem and testing various solutions, and for marketing it might be figuring out competitor strengths and weaknesses. It's important to determine the critical sub-tasks for each of the major performance objectives. It's not necessary for these to be completely SMARTe, but at a minimum they need to include the task, the primary action required, and a rough time frame. A simple sub-task for the SAP project could be *"Review the status of the current implementation for reasonableness and modify as necessary to meet the overall project requirements."*

Here are some questions hiring managers can use to help develop some of these sub-tasks:

1) *What kind of work will the person be doing most of the time?* – e.g., handling in-bound calls 50% of the time, making cold calls, writing code, supporting a production line.

2) *What are the biggest (technical) challenges or problems the person would need to address?* – e.g., figure out the failure modes for new electro-mechanical pumps, develop new consolidation techniques, write code to solve user-interface issues.

3) *What are the team issues or challenges?* Include who the person will work with regularly. – e.g., work with production and finance to develop cost data for the new product line.

4) *What are the key deliverables?* – e.g., get the product spec approved by March, submit monthly summaries of results.

5) *Are there any strategic or big-picture issues that need to be considered?* – e.g., work with operations to develop the long-term capacity plan.

6) *Are there any changes or improvements that need to be made?* – e.g., reduce costs in the admin department by 10% by year-end, improve factory yield from 97.5% to 99% in 90 days.

7) *What's a typical problem or the person is likely to face?* – hire four new program managers to handle rapid growth, product specs are not being met and customers are complaining.

Recruiters and candidates alike can ask these same questions to the hiring manager.

Another way to prepare performance profiles is to benchmark the performance of good people already doing the same job. To use this approach, first identify a few people who are considered top performers. Then determine what these people do on an ongoing basis that separates them from the average and the below-average performers. For a call center rep it might be perfect attendance or maintaining a positive attitude throughout the whole shift. For a sales rep benchmarking might reveal that the best reps always thoroughly understand their prospective clients' needs long before the initial live meeting. These differences can then be converted into performance objectives and included in the performance profile.

Preparing performance profiles as described doesn't take much time, but it has great value from an assessment standpoint. In addition, you won't need to interview as many people, since many will be screened out during the phone interview. This alone is a big time savings. You can also use the performance profile for onboarding and performance management purposes. During the onboarding process it's important to refine, reprioritize, and clarify the performance expectations for the job to make sure the new hire and hiring manager are on the same page. While the initial performance profile needs to be close, it can be adjusted somewhat based on the person ultimately hired. The performance profile can then be used throughout the year as a performance management and review tool.

It's best if this performance profile is created in steps, starting with a basic template like the following for a marketing product manager. Then get more people involved who will be working with the new hire to review the performance profile and add their comments. When you're done you can then prioritize the objectives in order of importance. This is a great way to get everyone on the hiring team to fully understand the job. This will be important as they interview candidates, since they'll all be using the same document to assess the person as well as describing the same job. Top people become concerned when the interviewers don't really know much about the job opening, or its importance.

First Draft of a Performance Profile for a Marketing Product Manager

1) Work with engineering and develop the product requirements document for the new iPad apps bundle. Target: 90 days.

2) Present the rough product road map to the executive team for review by June. Include primary product requirements and rough competitive analysis.

3) Identify additional marketing opportunities to grow sales to the $250k/month range by year-end.

4)   Establish yourself as an industry-wide subject matter expert on mobile user interface and usability.

Developing the Employee Value Proposition

As part of the performance profile process it's important to create the **Employee Value Proposition** (EVP). This describes what's in it for the candidate, by clarifying and defining in detail the reasons why a top person would take this job over other competing opportunities, including a counter-offer. This is a critical aspect of attracting top people. To understand and create the EVP, hiring managers need to think why a top person, who is not looking, or a person who has multiple opportunities, would want the job being offered at a modest increase in pay.

To get started with this, it helps to understand the intrinsic motivator of the "ideal candidate" to develop the EVP. One way is to ask top performers currently in the job to explain the source of their motivation to excel, or what they like most about the job. For technical people this is often applying their expertise in some unique way or learning a new skill. For aspiring managers and executives it could be the chance to make an important impact with success enabling them to accelerate their career growth. For health care workers the EVP is more likely something to do with helping their patients in some meaningful way. Good customer service people, including anyone who works directly with customers, typically derive satisfaction from providing exceptional service to others. All of these are intrinsic motivators (i.e., drivers of self-satisfaction). Note that the first two are about receiving a personal benefit, while the second two are giving a benefit to others. Regardless of intrinsic motivator, it's important to know it for the job opening under consideration since it will be incorporated into job postings, emails, and voicemails as a means to get top people excited about the opportunity.

A real example will help clarify how the EVP can be captured in the job posting. On a recent search assignment, we were targeting directors of accounting currently working at the corporate offices of the major entertainment companies in Los Angeles. Many of them want to get more hands-on so the EVP for this group was: get out of the trenches of accounting and work directly with line and production people producing next generation videos and TV shows for children around the world. The ad we created for this and posted on LinkedIn had this title "Oscar Winning Controller or Director of Accounting." There's a copy of the ad itself archived online. (http://budurl.com/AGcontAD)

Also note the format of the ad. Aside from the attention-grabbing title, Year One and Beyond are emphasized, with the skills and experience described in minimalist fashion at the end of the posting. Attracting top people using this type of Year One and Beyond format will increase the quality level of good people seen, since this is how they're making their career decisions.

There is no reason why you should be posting internal job descriptions as part of your external recruitment advertising. You wouldn't provide this type of information in a product advertisement to attract customers, so why would you do it for a job posting? Don't post the full performance profile either. Instead, extract the most important parts of the job and tell a story leading with the EVP, quickly highlighting the key projects, and a minimalist summary of the required skills. Top people reading the ad will then be able to instantly relate.

Continuing Benefits of Performance Profiles over Job Descriptions

Using performance profiles instead of traditional skills-based job descriptions has value not only in improving assessment accuracy, but also in helping the candidate better understand real job needs. Clarifying objectives up front has been shown to increase employee satisfaction, improve on-the-job performance, and reduce turnover. On this basis alone, using them as part of the hiring process makes logical sense, especially since traditional skills-based job descriptions offer none of these advantages. As part of this it's also important for getting everyone on the hiring team to base their evaluations on the same set of performance objectives. This alone will help reduce errors due to emotional bias, intuition, and lack of understanding of real job needs.

If you need more reasons to banish job descriptions from the hiring process, I wrote an article (http://budurl.com/banishLA) providing a bunch of other explanations why they prevent companies from hiring the best. The underlying rationale is based on understanding the career focus of the best people who are not looking. For one thing, they are not looking to gain more experience doing the same thing. Instead they want a chance to make an impact doing work they find satisfying. Most likely, they don't have the exact mix of experience and skills listed in the job description. Using performance profiles can help bridge this gap by defining what it takes to be successful, not simply listing the skills required. The point being, if you can find someone who has achieved success doing comparable things listed in the performance profile, they have exactly the right mix of experience and skills to do it at your company.

Why Managers Need to Make Time to Prepare Performance Profiles

Regardless of where we are in the world, recruiters frequently raise this all too-common complaint: *What do you do when a manager says he/she doesn't have time to prepare a performance profile?* The unstated implication behind this lack of direction from the hiring manager is that the recruiter should know the job requirements without having to be told. This is not true, but some managers believe it is. If you're a recruiter and have ever been confronted with this situation, here are some ideas to handle the reluctant manager:

1) Send them a copy of this book and have them read this chapter at least two or three times. This will work, sometimes.

2) Ask the manager when he or she will tell the person being hired what the job is all about. Rarely do you get a "never" with this question, and generally it's before the candidate starts. Under

this scenario, just ask the manager if it would make sense to tell you the same information so you won't have to meet people who aren't interested in doing the work.

3) Ask the manager if he or she would rather spend 30-40 minutes one time or spend 30-40 minutes extra every day urging the person hired who's not motivated to do the work required to do average work. Then point to a few people the manager's hired who are underperforming and require this extra supervision.

4) Put the manager on the defensive at the start of the meeting and ask why a top person who's not looking would be enticed to consider this job. In essence, start the discussion by forcing the hiring manager to create the EVP.

5) Look at the job description and say, this is not a job description at all. It's a person description. (Point: skills, experience, academics, and industry background describe a person, not a job.) Then say, let's put the job description in the parking lot and define the actual job first. If you're into logic, you might then say, skills and experiences are secondary criteria. They don't determine success, success determines the skills needed. Success is the primary criteria. So let's define success and we'll find people who are both competent and motivated to do this.

6) Ask the manager why people get promoted internally at your company. Most will say performance. Then point to a few people who got promoted on their performance, not their level of skills. Let this point sink in and then say, "Why don't we use the same measure to hire people from the outside? We can start by defining successful performance, and then we'll find people who have been successful doing similar work." Don't be surprised when you're not only seeing more top people, getting fewer top people saying they're not interested, and hiring more top people who have exactly the right level of skills and experiences to do the work required. Surprisingly, it will be about 70-80% of the stuff listed in the original job description, but in a different mix,

from different industries, with different academics, and with wide-ranging total years of experience.

As you'll discover after hiring a few top people using this approach, that it's what people DO with what they HAVE that matters, not what they HAVE in an absolute sense. Also since you're deemphasizing absolute levels of skills and experience, but not compromising on performance, you'll be able to consider a more diverse population of candidates. This is a huge benefit, aside from seeing and hiring more top people with far broader backgrounds and experiences.

The Legal Implications and Value of Using Performance Profiles Instead of Traditional Job Descriptions

There is a whitepaper summary in the Appendix prepared by David Goldstein of Littler Mendelson providing the general legal validation for using performance profiles versus job descriptions for compliance purposes. Rather than restate everything, following are the big points. The biggest of them all though is that performance profiles are far superior to traditional job descriptions if you want to hire stronger people, minimize legal compliance and discrimination claims, and increase assessment accuracy. Here are a few other key legal and compliance points:

- A properly prepared performance profile can identify and document the essential functions of a job better than traditional position descriptions, facilitating the reasonable accommodation of disabilities and making it easier to comply with the Americans with Disabilities Act and similar laws.

- Even employers that maintain more traditional job descriptions may still use performance profiles or summaries of performance profiles to advertise job openings. Employers are not legally required to post their internal job descriptions when advertising an open position. Nor is there any legal obligation to (or advantage in) posting boring ads.

- Under some circumstances, federal government contractors will want to include in their job postings, objective, non-comparative qualifications for the position to be filled. Using SMARTe, employers can create performance based job descriptions that include such objective, non-comparative elements. Requiring applicants to have previously accomplished specific tasks represents a selection criterion that is no less objective than requiring years of experience in some general area.

- Focusing on Year 1 and Beyond criteria may open the door to more minority, military, and disabled candidates who have a less "traditional" mix of experiences, thereby supporting affirmative action or diversity efforts.

Bottom line, performance profiles are more objective, more effective, and a more powerful approach for finding, assessing, recruiting, and hiring top talent. Continuing to rely on traditional skills-infested job descriptions will prevent companies from hiring enough top talent and reduce their overall business performance.

CANDIDATE ADVICE
How to Figure Out the Performance Profile

Most managers you meet will not be able to tell you many details about the performance objectives for the job. In this case, make sure that you ask everyone who interviews you to clarify job expectations. This includes the hiring manager, the recruiter, and everyone on the hiring team. There should be consistency among them. To get a sense of this right away, just ask the HR person or recruiter what the person in this role needs to accomplish in order to meet the performance objectives of the position. If they don't know, you have a clue as to how professional the company is and how closely the recruiter is working with the hiring manager. Good recruiters should understand the real requirements of the job. If they don't, recognize that they're largely just gatekeepers, judging you largely on your skills, experience, and personality.

In the chapter devoted fully to candidates and job hunting, some advice is offered on how to handle this situation. The key: don't be too eager, but ask enough relevant questions about the performance requirements of the job, so you have a chance to demonstrate some relevant prowess. The recruiter will need this information to recommend that you're seen by the hiring manager.

From a candidate's perspective the theme behind Performance-based Hiring is to clarify job expectations and provide the interviewer your best examples of comparable work. Use the SMARTe acronym to frame your responses, giving details for each of the letters (i.e., Specific, Measurable, Action taken, Results achieved, Time frame, and the environment). By asking each interviewer what they expect the person to do or accomplish, you'll be able to provide them with reasonable performance-based answers. If there is lack of consistency, address this with the recruiter or hiring manager. If there is conflict among the expectations, make sure you resolve this before ever considering taking the job, if offered. Bringing up the inconsistencies diplomatically will most likely be considered a positive.

As part of your personal assessment of the company and the opportunity, you should know what the top 4-5 performance expectations for the job are before even considering the opportunity seriously. If you don't, recognize that you're taking the job, if offered, for something other than career reasons. If the hiring manager hasn't fully thought through the performance requirements of the job, you'll be able to present a summary based on your conversations with all of the other interviewers. Your insight, if the summary is correct, should impress just about everyone, especially if you've presented convincing examples of doing comparable work successfully. Few candidates have the wherewithal to ask these types of questions. As a result, the few who do will be perceived as stronger candidates. More important, you'll understand how you'll be measured if you are offered the position and accept it.

....

Summary – Using Performance Profiles to Describe Real Job Needs

- **Use performance profiles to define the work rather than skills-infested job descriptions.** Having the skills listed on the job description doesn't guarantee success, but it does guarantee you won't see any good people who can do the work, but have a different mix of skills and experience. Unless the skills listed actually predict performance, they're counter-productive.

- **First determine what the person taking the job needs to do to be successful.** Preparing performance profiles is pretty easy. Just write down the most important things a person taking the job needs to do most of the time. Start with an action verb like build, design, improve, or maintain, and then describe the task. Then put the tasks in order of importance.

- **Be SMARTe.** Take each task and convert it into a SMARTe performance objective. By making the task Specific, Measurable, Action-based, Results-oriented, and Time-bound you'll be able to more accurately measure successful performance. Add something about the environment to ensure the right fit with the culture, the hiring manager's leadership style, the pace of decision-making, any resource limitations, unique challenges, and anything that could affect performance.

- **Convert HAVING to DOING.** Describe what the person needs to actually do with each skill, competency, or factor listed on the job description. Add these as tasks to the performance profile and make them as SMARTe as possible. This is a much better way to understand the importance of any skill and how to measure it.

- **Develop the employee value proposition (EVP) before you open the requisition.** You need to understand why a top person who's not looking would want your job for only a modest increase in pay. If you don't know the ideal candidate's intrinsic or career motivation behind taking your job, you're missing a great opportunity to attract more top-flight prospects without compensation being the primary incentive.

- **Performance profiles are an essential component of great management.** Clarifying expectations upfront is the primary driver of exceptional performance and job satisfaction. They can be used to not only find and hire great people, but retain them as well. They should also be used during the on-boarding process since they represent the front-end of a company's performance management system. Since managers promote people based on their performance, it's only logical that they should be hired on the same basis.

- **Performance profiles save time.** The primary reason otherwise competent people underperform is lack of motivation to do the actual work required. When people are measured on their absolute level of skills, their IQ or technical competence, their personality and level of assertiveness, rather than their ability and motivation to do the work required, it's unlikely they'll be successful. As retired corporate executive Red Scott once said, "Hire

smart, or manage tough." It takes a lot more time to moti-
vate and push people to achieve average performance than
it takes to prepare a performance profile.

- **Performance profiles are more legal.** While listing
  a specific degree or amount of experience required is
  objective, it doesn't mean it's accurate. If you're eliminating protected classes from consideration using traditional
  job descriptions, you could be exposing your company to
  unnecessary compliance and discrimination claims. If all
  candidates are assessed using the objectives listed in the
  performance profile, you'll not only open up the pool to
  more diverse and well-qualified candidates, but you'll also
  have a strong legal case to defend your hiring decisions.

- **Candidates need to create the performance profile
  during the first interview.** If the interviewer begins by
  asking a bunch of nonsensical questions or box checks
  your resume, diplomatically pause the conversation.
  Then ask the interviewer what the person taking this job
  needs to do to be considered successful. Your response
  needs to be examples of your best and most comparable
  accomplishments. Take about 2-3 minutes describing
  the accomplishment including specific details, examples
  of going the extra mile, who you worked with, and any
  recognition you received for doing good work. Entice the
  interviewer to ask you more questions about the accomplishment.

Chapter 7

Developing a Sourcing Strategy

Here's my big-picture perspective on sourcing: there's a right way, a wrong way, and everything else in between. Unfortunately, most companies try to improve the wrong way, and are satisfied with marginal improvements. In the long run, being bad doing the right things is a lot better than being good doing the wrong things. Of course, if you have a big employer brand and have a surplus of great people to choose from, sourcing is not the problem, selection is. This whole book, especially the two chapters on sourcing, will help everyone else find great people, too. Collectively the process of sourcing the right way begins by being candidate and prospect focused.

Good Sourcing Begins by Matching to How Top People Look for New Careers

The following checklist is a guide to what's covered in the next two chapters on sourcing. You might find the process similar to preparing a traditional consumer marketing plan focused on identifying the needs and desires of a target customer. In this case of hiring, the target customer is the ideal, or perfect, candidate. Every marketing plan begins with a strategy and the development of a customer profile. This is also a critical step for finding and hiring top people. Then the plan needs to get into specifics: understanding buying patterns, preparing advertising copy, identifying target customers, identifying the best channels to reach these people, and concluding with the actual engagement and selling techniques. And just like every consumer marketing and sales plan, it needs to be different for each unique product and customer. I suggest that developing a plan like this should be prepared for every unique job you're trying to fill. Timing is equally as important – before you start looking for people to fill the job.

Whether you need to find 500 people, or just one person to fill a critical role, here's a step-by-step guide for developing a customized sourcing plan to find perfect candidates:

A Checklist for Developing a Customized Sourcing Plan

Chapter 7 – High-level Strategy and Planning

❑ Don't use the wrong talent strategy to find the right candidates. The point: you can't use a surplus sourcing model to find and hire people in a Scarcity of Talent situation.

❑ Understand your "ideal" candidate before you start looking. Preparing a candidate persona is the key to this.

❑ Be an early adopter. Many new sourcing programs actually work quite well, at least until everyone else begins using them. Playing follow-the-leader is a sure way to miss out on some of the best candidates.

❑ Become an Early-bird to contact the best candidates before everyone else. This starts by understanding what motivates top people to look for other jobs, giving you the tools and insight needed to attract them before they start looking, or on they day they start their new job search.

❑ Reverse-engineer your job posting process. If the best people can't find you, it doesn't matter what you're offering.

Chapter 8 – Detailed Sourcing Plans and Tactics

❑ Implement a 20/20/60 Sourcing Plan. Targeting the total talent market of active and passive candidates requires a combination of hand and power tools and techniques.

❑ Conduct a supply vs. demand analysis to first understand the depth of the sourcing challenge and the approach required.

❑ Use Recruitment Marketing 101 concepts to attract the best. The key: offer career moves instead of lateral transfers. There is no law that says you need to post skills-infested, boring job descriptions. Converting these into compelling career stories will change the mix of people you see.

❑ Add the "Two-step" apply process to weed out the weak and excite the best. The "apply" button comes in many colors and shapes. There's no need for yours to be a black empty hole that people see right in your job posting.

❑ Be clever at Boolean. Adding achiever terms to simple search strings will bring the top 25% to the top of your list. Combining these with appropriate demographic and diversity keywords will allow you to begin finding the exact candidates you need within a few hours after opening the requisition.

❑ Use social media to create Virtual Talent Communities. A virtual talent community is represented by your connections' connections. With LinkedIn Recruiter you're able to search on these connections and proactively ask about these people, rather than hoping someone refers them.

❑ Push personalized emails to your target list before the sun sets. Maximize your email response rate by capturing your ideal candidate's career motivator in the Subject and the first line. Candidates will respond the next day when it's done quickly and professionally.

❑ Go slow, as fast as you can. For passive candidates, don't sell the job, sell the next step – a short discussion about a possible career move. This is not only how you'll get everyone to talk to you, but also how to build a deep network of top talent for your next assignment.

Great sourcing begins with understanding your "ideal" candidate, developing career-oriented messaging, and finding the most direct route to get it to them. Most people use some type of indirect means to find talented people, hoping a good candidate will fall through the cracks. As a result, time-to-fill and Quality of Hire are problematic, since these are dependent on when a person acceptable to the hiring manager applies. Since true cost per hire is largely a function of time, this is also an uncontrolled dependent variable. Posting boring ads emphasizing lateral transfers, waiting for a great person who has an economic need to apply, and then having to endure your company's ill-conceived obstacle course is the wrong way to find and hire great talent on a consistent basis. Defining Quality of Hire and targeting these people directly, either via networking or pushing career-oriented messaging to them, is the right way. It doesn't matter if the person is active or passive, the message and the distribution channel is what matters. In the process Quality of Hire becomes the driving objective, and if done efficiently with appropriate process control metrics, you'll also be able to minimize time-to-fill and as a result, cost per hire.

Most recruiting leaders don't think about their sourcing problems this way. Instead, most focus on finding the next sourcing silver bullet and waiting for someone else to prove it before they venture into waters unknown. The problem here is that once everyone has it, it's no longer silver. Despite the obvious futility of chasing the leader while chasing your tail, the search for the next sourcing silver bullet is still relentlessly pursued.

I've been sourcing top candidates for 35 years, and in all those years and various economic climates, I have never had a problem finding enough good candidates quickly. The key has always been using whatever tools exist, using them first to gain first-user benefits, and then later, executing better than everyone else. As long as you address and solve the problem this way, it won't matter what new sourcing ideas come along. When they do you'll be able to gain an early user competitive advantage and maintain your lead through constant improvement. Under this approach you'll be able to successfully handle whatever hiring challenge comes along.

CANDIDATE ADVICE
Take Every Call From a Recruiter

....

Recruiters are nodes too, so building a network of connections, including well-placed recruiters, is an important aspect of any job-hunting effort. However, the bad: everybody already does this, so you need to be creative to get noticed and you must reinforce the relations, not just be a nuisance. I still get lots of people who call me and tell me they're looking for a job. I don't recall taking any of these calls, unless the person was referred to me from a highly regarded person, or the person was someone who could help me in some way in the future.

The idea behind this is that recruiters find people for jobs they're working on. They're not in the business to find jobs for people.

So if you're well-connected and can help the recruiter find some other good people, it's worth setting up a conversation. Giving the recruiter some good referrals will help the relationship. Of course, the best time to do this is when you're not looking. They'll then return the favor to the degree possible when you are job-hunting. So take every call from a recruiter and never say you're not interested. It's best to build your future job-hunting network when you're not looking for a job.

The Inbound vs. Outbound Difference between Active and Passive Candidates

From a sourcing standpoint, recruitment advertising programs need to be set up so that active candidates can find you. This is an inbound process. It's different for passive candidate. In this case, you need to seek them out. This is an outbound process. In either case, once contact is made the primary objective is to convince the person of the merits of what you have to offer. Some of the convincing is incorporated in the written messages, sometimes it's on the phone. Regardless, the inbound vs. outbound difference is important when thinking about and developing sourcing programs.

THE RECRUITING FUNNEL

Measuring and Managing Yield at Each Step Maximizes Hiring Success

From an inbound active candidate standpoint, being better at attracting more top active candidates means you need to be both found and compelling. From an outbound passive candidate standpoint, finding and attracting more top passive candidates is largely about aggressive networking in combination with compelling career messaging. These are either pushed to the desk of worthy prospects or to people who are directly connected to them.

The recruiting funnel shown in the diagram can help you visualize this inbound vs. outbound difference and the process used to convert contacts into candidates and ultimately into great hires. The most obvious point is that if there aren't enough good people at the top of the funnel to begin with, there won't be many left at the end to hire. So yield (conversion rate at each step) and the quality of the candidate pool are both important. Yield is less important for attracting average active candidates, more important for recruiting the best active candidates, and vital for recruiting passive candidates. If you're not measuring the quality level of your prospect pool at the top of the funnel, and yield at every step in the process, you're missing a great opportunity to hire more great people primarily due to lack of process control. An example will help illustrate the importance of this "quality at the top" concept.

One of our recent projects involved working with a fast-growing Russian high-tech company. As part of this work, I had the head of their product management group walk me through his hiring process. Due to rapid growth, the company needed to hire 2-3 people per quarter into the department, so this was an on-going and important activity that was not working too well. His basic approach involved searching through a resume database of tens of thousands and filtering it down to 1,000 people who had technical degrees from the best Russian universities. He then winnowed this group down further to 100 people to contact and screen, and then invited 25 to interview. From this he had 2-3 finalists, but struggled to find even one to hire. Then he started the process over again. While the process seemed reasonable, the results were dismal.

To figure out the problem, I suggested we first look at 50 or so resumes from the pre-selected target group of 1,000. It was hard to find one strong performer in the group who met all his qualifications. The initial conclusion was that he was probably using the wrong database to start the search process. However, as we discussed the job, it was my opinion that the job was less technical and more project management-oriented. Using this broader filter we found a number of high-achievers in the initial database who seemed better suited for the job. With a better group to select from at the top of the funnel, the results at the bottom were obviously better, too. The point here is that the filters he used to develop the initial target pool were too narrow, and he wasted time and resources applying a good screening process to the wrong starting point. The same logic holds when posting an ad. If your ad is compelling, and at the top of the search listings, but no one reasonable applies, stop posting the same ad in the same place.

Yield is a different problem. Yield tracks the success rate of converting a strong person into someone who's interested in what you have to offer, qualifying the person, getting the person to apply, and ultimately into a person who accepts your offer. Managing yield starts with the principle that the best people are looking for career moves, not lateral transfers. Obviously the better the job from a career perspective, the more people will be interested, and the yield will be higher. The key to managing yield is the need to minimize people voluntarily opting out of your process until they have enough facts to determine whether your opening represents a true career move or not. This is one of the critical skills recruiters need to master to maximize the number of passive candidates ultimately hired. If you're not tracking yield at each step in the hiring process, you'll never be able to figure out if you have a problem or not, much less improve it.

With the objective of improving end-to-end yield and increasing productivity, following are the core things to do before you even start looking for top candidates. If you don't do these front-end things, whatever else you do will be inefficient, ineffective, or short-lived. This has to do with the wrong way vs. right way premise introducing this chapter.

Are You Operating Under a Talent Scarcity or Talent Surplus Strategy?

If the demand for talent is greater than the supply, you can't use a process that's based on the premise that the supply is greater than the demand. You should recognize that you are using a surplus of talent approach if you post boring jobs and spend most of your time weeding out unqualified candidates. The hope with this approach is that a few good candidates will remain standing at the end. This is okay if you're seeing and hiring enough top people on a consistent basis for your critical positions. If not, the underlying strategy is flawed. In this case it doesn't matter what sourcing tools you use, you'll waste time and resources looking for the needle in the haystack. It might be better to start looking for these needles in different haystacks. Since the talent strategy concept was covered in great depth in Chapter 1, there's no need to repeat it here. What is important is to recognize what default strategic hiring model your company is using. If you answer yes or true to most of the following, you are operating under a surplus strategy:

❑ We post traditional skills and experience-based job descriptions.

❑ Our hiring managers are not fully engaged in the hiring process.

❑ Our recruiters are more concerned with productivity than quality.

❑ Our legal or IT department determines how we write ads.

❑ Our comp department determines what we pay our candidates, even the stars.

❑ Our basic approach is "one size fits all," meaning there is very little that's unique or customized for the position.

❑ Critical positions are treated on an exception basis.

❑ The only career information in our job postings is company boilerplate and PR-speak.

❑ We don't have a "Raising the Talent Bar" program in place ensuring short-term manager needs are balanced with long-term company talent goals.

❑ We often exclude great people because they're too light, or someone has conducted a superficial interview.

❑ We use an informal assessment and selection process with many interviewers conducting short interviews (30-40 minutes or less).

❑   Most of our candidates have responded to our job postings
     rather than through aggressive networking and referral
     programs.

The key point: if you're using a hiring process that is based on the
existence of an excess supply of good people for a specific job, it won't
work if the assumption is wrong. The following sourcing ideas will help
a little, but these are just short-term fixes; the real problem is the wrong
strategy.

Developing the Candidate Persona

In addition to knowing the job, you also need to understand your ideal
candidate before you start looking. The Candidate Persona form in the
Appendix is used as part of our Recruiter Boot Camp (http://budurl.
com/RBCOnew) training course. I suggest that the recruiter and the
hiring manager prepare this form and the performance profile together.
The candidate persona will help everyone understand these three big
things about the ideal candidate, plus a lot of little ones:

•   Whether the person is active or passive

•   What the person needs to know in order to consider
    switching jobs

•   How to find the person most quickly

As you review the form, you'll see all of the information is needed to
find the person, and what type of information is needed to attract and
convince the person that your opportunity is worth pursuing.

THE CANDIDATE PERSONA

Key Factors to Consider	Comments	Ideas and Comments
What is candidate looking for in a new job?	Career move, a better job or a lateral transfer	
What phase of job-hunting process is ideal candidate likely to be in?	Explorer, Tiptoer, Googler, Networker, Hunter, Talent Pool	
Types of jobs previously held	Consider growth of candidate position to position	
Build 360° network	Who would have worked with the candidate	
Direct & functional competitors	Consider vendors or non-competitive firms	
Comparative titles	Consider every type of title imaginable	
Candidate SEO terms	What terms would a candidate use to Google for the job?	
Recognition and Achiever terms	Consider awards & recognition likely for this type of person	
Professional societies & groups	What groups does the person join on LinkedIn? Is the person a member of yours?	
Demographic or diversity terms	Consider special groups or keywords	
Personal advisory team	Who will help person decide & what info do they need?	
Primary selection criteria	What factors will they use to compare positions?	
Underlying long term motivation of a top performer	What value would drive this person to respond & consider?	

Describe Your "Ideal" Candidate Before You Begin Searching

Much of the information on the form will be used throughout this section whether you're searching for resumes, writing emails and job postings, or talking with the person on the phone. Whenever you take a new assignment ask the hiring manager for help with completing the form or talk with people already in the role. This information will help you find your ideal candidate more quickly and more efficiently.

Early Adopters and Early-birds Enjoy a Huge Competitive Advantage

Early adopters and Early-birds have two totally different meanings when it comes to finding prospects and candidates for your job openings:

- Early adopters refer to those people who are willing to try and buy new products, ideas, or services before anyone else.

- Early-birds are recruiters who find candidates before everyone else, even before the candidates start looking or the moment they do.

While I sometimes dismiss many new sourcing tools as just more of the same, this is not universally true. Some of these tools are quite good and very useful for those who get access to them first. Many are different enough to reach a different group of people. Some are actually temporary silver bullets. Getting access to a new pool of prospects and candidates before everyone else is a real advantage. For example, the first group of people who used job boards had great success, even when posting boring ads.

However, once everyone had access to the same job boards, their success reverted to the mean: getting average results. To continue to get good results you then had to make sure you were at the top of the listing and stood out in some way. When job aggregators became available, the early adopters had great success followed by diminishing returns as everyone else hopped on board.

The point here is that early adopters have a distinct advantage just by being first, even if their subsequent processes were less than ideal. The other point is that later adopters can still obtain value from these new sourcing channels if they execute better. This means their postings are easily found, their job titles stand out in some way, and their postings are compelling, not reprints of their internal job descriptions. There's more on how to do this below, but for now, I'd suggest everyone adopt an early-adopter mentality. Don't wait for other companies to tell you how great these new sourcing ideas are before you decide to take the plunge. By then it will be too late, and you'll wonder what all the fuss was about.

Use an Early-bird Sourcing Strategy

An Early-bird Sourcing strategy, on the other hand, is much more important and much more effective for finding and hiring top talent on a consistent basis, especially for those who aren't looking. This is shown in the accompanying diagram. This chart has been prepared in conjunction with LinkedIn and is based on multiple surveys of their members. It requires a bit of explanation to fully understand and appreciate its value.

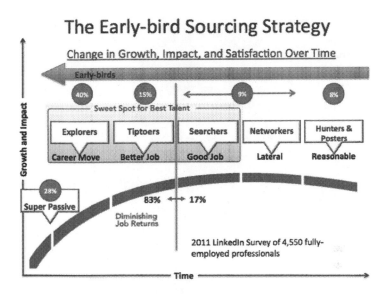

Finding Candidate Before Everyone Else is a
Huge Competitive Hiring Advantage

The curved line represents the typical growth and satisfaction level of a person over an extended period, typically years. Assuming the person took the right job, the person is learning a great deal and making an early impact. This is shown as the steep part of the curve on the left. As time goes on, and growth, learning, and impact slow down – as shown by a flattening of the curve – satisfaction with the job typically declines. This does not mean the person is actively looking, but it does indicate the person might be open to evaluate a job that might be better. If job growth and satisfaction continues to decline – the right hand portion of the curve – the person is more likely to actively seek another job. A lot of variables affect these decisions to consider something else, including the overall economy, the demand for the person's skills, the person's income and family needs, and the person's tolerance for risk vs. security.

Knowing where your ideal candidate falls on this curve is important for developing a sourcing plan. If the person is passive (those to the left of the diminishing returns line) you shouldn't use the same programs, processes, and techniques, to find and attract people who are more active (those on the right). This represents the tipping point from passive to active and is shown as the 83% vs. 17% dividing line on the diagram.

The curved line is also divided into six broad segments. Each is based on how satisfied the person is with their current job and what the person would likely require to switch jobs. These are described below with the percentages indicating the segment's size in comparison to the total. These group size percentages were developed from the survey data.

Super Passive (28% of the total sample): These people are absolutely not looking and aren't the least bit interested in talking with a recruiter except for networking purposes. However, while extremely satisfied, many would at least discuss a major move with a big equity stake or huge compensation increase.

Explorers (40%): These people are mostly satisfied with their current jobs and are not looking, but they are openly willing to explore an opportunity if it represented a clear career move. These are the classic passive candidates who need to be directly contacted by a recruiter and convinced that the opening is one worth considering. Much of the content in this book has been designed to find and attract this group.

Tiptoers (15%): These are people who are generally satisfied with their jobs, but recognize that there could be better career options available elsewhere. Tiptoers enter the first stage of job hunting by contacting their close former co-workers to see if they know of anything available at their companies. Partly this is due to the need to keep their job-hunting efforts private. At this stage they are looking for something much better than their current position by only contacting those who know them well and would vouch for their performance.

Searchers (approx. 5%): When people start looking seriously, at least if they're still working, they tend to first go to Google or a job aggregator (Indeed or SimplyHired) to see what's available. Using Google they'll add the term "jobs" with some title and some location to see what the job market is like. Very few companies are listed on the first few pages, mostly jobs from the aggregators or third-party agencies. Since they've just started looking, they are looking for a good job, something a little better than what they now have, not just a lateral transfer. To reach Searchers you'll need to be at the top of the listings with compelling titles, or else your job will be lost in the shuffle.

Networkers (approx. 4%): People are unwilling to start contacting people who aren't close former associates unless they need to get more aggressive in their job hunting efforts. By this stage their job hunting efforts are now more public. Even if they're employed, there are probably some dark clouds on the horizon, so they want to seriously begin looking. Under this economic need these people are less discriminating and would seriously consider a lateral transfer with some longer term security or other upside benefits.

Hunters and Posters (8%): Even if fully employed, it's probably in some sub-par position, one that is unsatisfying, or one that is short-lived. An economic need is driving their job-hunting efforts and they are open to consider any reasonable position.

While there are some good people in each of the groups, most of the best ones get picked up earlier in the process. This is what is meant by implementing an Early-bird Sourcing strategy. There are specific sourcing tactics you can use to get the best results for each of the phases. A sourcing plan begins by first figuring out what the most likely job-hunting phase is for your ideal candidate, and then developing your programs based on this.

For example, if you're in a talent shortage condition you'll likely need to target Explorers and Tiptoers. You'll be able to find Explorers using tools like LinkedIn Recruiter (http://budurl.com/LIRguide) coupled with strong recruiting and networking skills. You'll be able to find Tiptoers by leveraging your employee referral program. The best way to find people as soon as they enter the job market is to make sure your postings can be found on the first page of a Google search. This is why Search Engine Optimization is so important. CareerBuilder and Jobs2Web are leaders in this field. With their help, you'll be able to get active candidates before everyone else just by being at the top of the search listings.

One way to see how well your sourcing programs are working is to ask every candidate you talk with how long they've been looking and what techniques they've been using. If the person says, "I just started looking," or, "I'm not really looking yet; someone at your company contacted me," you're in good shape. If they say, "I've been looking for a few weeks," or more, you've got to wonder why it took so long for the person to find your posting. This is a great clue that your active candidate sourcing programs are inadequate.

Explorers, Tiptoers, and Searchers represent the "Sweet Spot" for finding top talent. Collectively they represent approximately 60% of the total pool of fully employed professionals. Surprisingly, most companies spend most of their time, effort, and resources targeting the 8% of candidates who are driven by an economic need to find a job – the Hunters. While there are some good people in this group, there are better ways to find them. In addition there are many other good candidates you need to consider as well. To do this you need to start with a Scarcity of Talent strategy emphasizing Early-bird Sourcing in the Sweet Spot.

CANDIDATE ADVICE
On Developing a Job-Hunting Strategy

....

Reverse engineer the Early-bird Sourcing process by completing the candidate persona for yourself. You'll need much of this information as you implement the step-by-step tactics described in the next chapter. Make sure you know what you're looking for in a new job and who you can connect to if you're a Tiptoer or Networker. Think about the positions you've had and their generic titles. This will be very helpful as you begin your search for jobs, either on Google or one of the job board aggregators like Simplyhired. com or Indeed.com. Most important of all, make sure all of your Achiever and recognition terms are readily found in your LinkedIn profile and any public resumes you've posted. In the next chapter I provide techniques for recruiters to search on these terms, so you'll want them to find you this way.

There is a lot more specific advice in the next chapter, but completing the candidate persona for yourself will get you started thinking about your job-hunting process from a different perspective. If you're actively seeking a new job, you'll need to be more proactive than just sending out resumes and waiting for a reply. This is the least effective way to find a new job. The most effective way is to connect with people who can vouch for you and get them to recommend you for a position at their company. LinkedIn will show you these connections when you search for a position on their site, so take advantage of this capability by expanding your network right away.

If you're a passive candidate who wants to eventually be found you'll want to start by making sure your LinkedIn profile is current and first rate. Then you'll want to start building a strong network of everyone you've worked closely with in the past, especially those who are strong supporters. Sometime in the future they'll either call you when they hear about a great career opportunity or you'll call them when you need help to get connected with some-one they know. In the interim, make sure you go out of your way to help them whenever needed.

Big point: getting a better job is more about finding someone who can personally vouch for you and recommend you directly to the hiring manager or recruiter working the search than it is about applying to an open position.

Summary – Developing a Sourcing Strategy

- Use the recruiting funnel to manage your sourcing pro-cesses. Track quality of candidate and yield if you want to improve each stage of your company's sourcing, recruit-ing, interviewing, and hiring processes. If you're not attracting enough top people at the top of the funnel it doesn't matter if your processes are good or bad, you won't hire anyone worth hiring. If you are attracting enough good people, you need to make sure none of them opt out without a full understanding of the career opportunity available.

- Do not use a talent-surplus strategy in a talent-scarcity sit-uation. If the demand for talent is greater than the supply, you need to implement proactive and creative recruitment marketing programs. The job postings themselves must be compelling and appeal to the intrinsic motivators of top people who have multiple opportunities. These mes-sages must clearly describe career growth, not just be an auto-posting of your company's internal job descriptions.

- Define your ideal candidate using the candidate persona as a guide. Great people don't look for work the same way average people do. And if they're fully-employed and sat-isfied they don't look at all. Understanding how to reach these people whether they're looking or not, and what to say to get them excited, is the first step of an effective talent acquisition program. Consider the candidate persona as equivalent to preparing a customer profile for marketing any product.

- Become an Early Adopter. While not all new sourcing tools are effective, some of them are. Regardless, they should all be seriously evaluated. For example, Career-Builder's Talent Network offers a quick means to build an instant talent pipeline, Webshark is building custom talent communities for companies in Europe, and LinkedIn is now offering analytical tools to conduct supply/demand for different jobs in different areas. Don't wait for others to try tools like this out before you invest, or you'll often wind up with average results as diminishing returns set in. As a guideline, be bold and be first. The worst that can happen is that you won't hire as many people as hoped, but in most cases you'll hire some.

- Implement an Early-bird Sourcing Strategy. Start asking all of your candidates how long they've been looking. If you're not finding candidates during their first week of job-hunting, it means your postings are invisible. If you want to see and hire the best, you want to find them before everyone else. This is a huge competitive advantage, since everyone else has to play catch-up.

- Candidates: start networking rather than applying. The probability of finding a job by applying to an ad is far less than finding someone who knows the recruiter or hiring manager and can recommend you. In the short-run, it's important to find people you know at the company running an ad of interest. Hopefully they'll recommend you and put you at the top of the list. In the long run, build and maintain your professional network on LinkedIn. This will probably be how you'll get your next great job.

Chapter 8

Sourcing Tactics, Tools & Techniques

The previous chapter focused on developing an appropriate sourcing strategy by understanding your target audience and their specific job-hunting needs. This chapter will describe some tools and techniques you can use to implement whatever strategy you decide is most appropriate. In general, I advocate a balanced 20/20/60 Sourcing Plan to ensure you're reaching the total pool of potential candidates.

The 20/20/60 Sourcing Plan to Find Anyone, Anywhere

The pie chart shown is a slightly different version of the Early-bird Sourcing graph shown in the previous chapter. This one presents the individual job-hunting categories as a percentage of the total talent pool. A 20/20/60 Sourcing Plan is designed to map to this talent mix ensuring you're considering all of the best people available, not just those who apply.

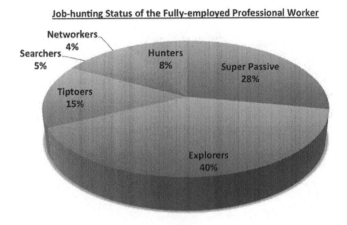

The 20/20/60 Sourcing Plan Covers the Full Talent Market

Specifically:

- **20% Focused on Compelling and Visible Postings:** The first 20% of your sourcing efforts should target active candidates using a combination of search engine optimized job postings in combination with compelling advertising. This will ensure you're targeting all of the Hunters, Networkers, and Searchers, and a few Tiptoers who are on the margin.

- **20% Focused on Name Generation and Targeted Emails:** The second 20% of your sourcing programs need to be pushed emails and InMails (LinkedIn's built-in email system) to reach Tiptoers and Explorers. You'll use some clever Boolean techniques to develop the target lists in combination with a robust CRM (Candidate Relationship Marketing) system to send the emails and track responses.

- **60% Focused on Direct Calling, Networking and Obtaining Pre-qualified Referrals:** The bulk of your sourcing efforts, the remaining 60%, needs to be networking-based, focused on finding the best Tiptoers, Explorers and possibly a few open-minded Super Passives. This requires the use of advanced recruiting techniques and the development of Virtual Talent Communities (VTC). A virtual talent community is comprised of your first degree LinkedIn connections and their connections. Using the advanced networking techniques described here, you'll be able find highly qualified prospects in a few days.

Start Each Search with a Supply vs. Demand Analysis of the Local Labor Market

A balanced 20/20/60 Sourcing Plan ensures full coverage of the total talent market, reaching both active and passive candidates using a variety of approaches. To determine which sourcing approach needs to be emphasized you should begin each new search project by conducting a supply vs. demand analysis. CareerBuilder's supply/demand talent portal (http://budurl.com/cbportal) is a good place to start. This tool compares the number of open jobs in an area to the number of candidates in their internal resume database and in accessible public resume databases. While it's a rough assessment, it does provide enough information to suggest that you might need to consider finding people from out of the area or investing in some more aggressive passive candidate recruiting efforts. I do something similar using LinkedIn Recruiter, comparing the number of total similar jobs being advertised to the number of total qualifying members in the same geography. LinkedIn also offers their own talent pool analysis (http://budurl.com/EGtalent)

for different high demand jobs in high demand areas. You could also sample your company's resume database to see if the quality mix meets your hiring standards.

If the supply of talent appears adequate, you might be able to find enough good candidates just through more visible and compelling advertising. On the other hand, if the labor market is tight, you'll then need to develop new processes for expanding the sourcing pool targeting both Tiptoers and Explorers.

Passive Candidate Recruiting Involves Big Changes

Recognize that once you venture into the passive candidate waters you can't use the same techniques to source and recruit these people as you do for active candidates. Here are the big changes you must implement before sourcing passive candidates:

1) Hiring managers must be fully engaged and supportive. This means they are willing to talk with a prospect on an exploratory basis, even if the person is not yet fully committed to the idea of formally applying for the job. The hiring manager's role in this discussion is to not only describe the job and understand what the person brings to the table, but also to convince the person that it's worth coming onsite for a full interview.

2) In a talent-scarcity situation, do not even think of using traditional job descriptions for advertising purposes. A performance profile coupled with the EVP are essential first steps. From this you'll be able to generate career-oriented job descriptions for your postings and emails.

3) Slow down the rush to close. Sourcing, recruiting, and hiring passive candidates for career moves is not a transactional process. It's a much different process than finding candidates to fill an open position. Recognize that the candidate needs to switch from a Day 1 decision-making mode to a Year 1 and Beyond

perspective. Equally important, recruiters must be able to Bridge the Gap on first contact to ensure prospects don't dismiss the job without a full understanding of the career opportunity your position offers.

A supply vs. demand analysis plus some actual results from your postings will help you develop the best sourcing channel mix. The overriding goal of your sourcing efforts should be to maximize Quality of Hire in the shortest time frame at the least cost. For example, if you can find enough good candidates immediately after posting your job, this should suffice. On the other hand, if the demand for a specific group of people is very high, the emphasis should be on networking. Regardless of your mix emphasis great execution on all fronts is important. Let's begin.

The First 20 – Compelling Advertising that Stands Out from the Humdrum Crowd

The first 20 in the 20/20/60 Sourcing plan is focused on finding great candidates using compelling advertising. The first part of this requires that the advertising or message itself is found by the right person. A great ad than no one reads is a total wasted effort. Even a bad ad that is seen and attracts some attention is a better outcome. A great ad that's found though, is a winning combination that will have great people ready and willing to apply. It starts by getting the compelling part figured out first.

Write Compelling Ads Rather Than Reposting Internal Job Descriptions

While being found is important, an ad is unlikely to be clicked on and read by a fully-employed Searcher unless your company has a well-known and positive employer brand. Few companies fall into this category. If not, you need something else to ensure your posting stands out from the crowd.

I can't understand why companies continue to post jobs that are boring, with an emphasis on skills and experience and a format that looks like everyone else's, and then wonder why they're not attracting any top people. This might work when the supply of great people is greater than the demand, but ineffective when the situation is reversed. The common job posting process is flawed, with job ads generally only found by people who are underemployed or have an economic need to find a worthy job. Since many job postings are pushed to a target audience (e.g., LinkedIn and Facebook), it's unlikely a top person will apply if the job appears to be a lateral transfer or the emphasis is on the "must have" skills and experiences listed. Despite this situation, the underlying and unstated hope is that a high-achiever will miraculously apply, be willing to endure the bureaucratic and demeaning maze that follows, and if an offer is made, be willing to accept a lateral transfer. Of course, when the ad doesn't generate any good people, the idea is to make the qualifications more stringent and post the same boring job in more places. It's hard to believe someone actually thought of this process, and harder still to believe people think it's a good idea.

As you apply the 20/20/60 mix approach, here's a simple sourcing rule to follow: if your job posting doesn't attract talented people, *don't use it anymore*! However, some sourcer/recruiter will put up a fight, contending that they need some way to screen out the unqualified. Somehow they miss the point that the process also screens out the most qualified. Preparing performance profiles, getting hiring managers to focus on performance over experience, and writing compelling ads that can be found solves this "wrong mix of candidates" problem.

One aspect of preparing performance profiles was to make sure the employee value proposition (EVP) was clearly understood, stated, and visible in your posting. The following real ad for a controller is one example. The EVP describes why a top person would take the job even if fully employed. The EVP covers what the person would learn, do, and become if successful. Describing what's in it for the candidate must be evident in the job posting and it must be included at the top of the posting where it's read first. Better: if you can get it into your first line, it will more likely appear in the Google listing.

Capturing the candidate's intrinsic motivator in the EVP statement is the goal of good recruitment advertising. The intrinsic motivator represents the fundamental reason why a person would leave a good job and consider yours superior. The EVP should be defined as part of developing the candidate persona for your ideal candidate. For passive candidates it's typically a bigger job with more stretch, a chance to make a bigger impact, a job that is personally more satisfying, or one with an opportunity to grow at a faster rate than the person's current situation. Sometimes the EVP is driven by eliminating a problem, like having a weak manager, lack of enough resources to do the job properly, or feeling disrespected or unfulfilled. For those with a technical focus the intrinsic motivator is typically tied to working on something important or being on the leading edge of technology. For people actively looking, the focus might be on security or economic issues, or finding a job that offers a better work/life balance. Regardless of the motivator, it's important that you know it and capture it in your job posting. The intrinsic motivator underlying the controller position was an opportunity to get out of the numbers and work with line operations helping them run their business better. Not all accounting people want this, but this was critical for on-the-job success for the specific job described.

Use Advertising to Attract the Best, Not Weed Out the Weak

Job Description

If you want to accelerate your career growth, you need to stop thinking about the day one stuff. Instead, think year one, and beyond.

For example, take this search we're now working on. It involves a small LA/Valley-based entertainment company that's asked us to find them a finance and admin executive to help them become as big as their dreams. As a result, you will, too! That's the stuff that's beyond year one.

If you're interested, here's what year one is all about. For a CPA, this is the stuff of dreams – getting out of the numbers and making a difference.

- Upgrade every single accounting process and procedure, including the entire reporting process. As part of this, make sure the internal controls are as tight as a drum.
- Take over and rebuild the admin side of the company including procurement, contracts, funding and legal. You'll be working closely with studio and production people, so you need to speak non-accounting.
- Rebuild the budgeting and planning process, including corporate reporting, and lead the preparation of the annual operating plan.
- Prepare a monthly analysis and reporting package that identifies what's really happening in the company. Cool charts and graphs would help.

Realistically, we need someone with a CPA (there's a bunch of public reporting and tax issues involved), and an MBA would add a lot of credibility. Most important is a hands-on understanding of the weird entertainment industry accounting treatments associated with a dozen independent collaborators involved in every production. If you pull all this off, all the folks you'll be working with will be thanking you when they receive their Oscars and Emmys.

While this is all of the Year One and Beyond stuff, Day One is pretty good, too. These are things like the compensation, the company, the people, and the location. However, none of this matters unless "Year One and Beyond" makes career sense for you.

Desired Skills & Experience

If you can accomplish the above, you've got what it takes. Realistically though, you need a CPA or CMA. If you have an MBA on top of this, you'll be able to accelerate your effectiveness and impact. Hands-on knowledge of the entertainment industry accounting issues is really important. If you have it, you know why. If you don't, ask someone who does, and if they think you can do the work, or they'll help you through it, let's talk anyway.

Emphasize the Job-hunting Needs of the "Ideal Candidate"

Look at the sample ad above to get an idea of a good structure for a job posting. The first thing you'll notice is that it's not a rehash of either the job description (a super big no-no) or the performance profile (which is still a no-no, but not as big).

Rather than post the job description or performance profile, the posting tells a compelling story that's designed to appeal to the target candidate. As part of this story, you'll notice there are four main elements:

1) A compelling or unusual title. This is used to stand out in the search listing.

2) The EVP is somewhere near the top. It's always best to lead off the recruitment advertising with the big benefit for considering the job, like future growth or bigger impact or a more exciting job. (Note: this is basic marketing, i.e., "Sell the benefits, not the specifications.")

3) A quick summary of the big tasks and projects. In the sample ad there are four projects listed in quick summary form. These were taken directly from the performance profile for the job, with a bit of explanation describing how they fit in with the company's business and why they're important. These are Year 1 performance objectives. They represent what the person will be doing or working on much of the time. Clarifying expectations this way, even roughly, is far more meaningful than listing a bunch of skills and required experiences.

4) Minimize the skills and experience requirements, but describe how they'll be used on the job, rather than as a demeaning list of screen-out requirements, which is a huge turnoff. The sample ad states that the company needs a CPA to handle all of the international consolidation and SEC reporting requirements. This is much more compelling and meaningful than saying, "Must have a CPA, must have 5+ years of experience in international reporting, and must have a strong background and experience preparing SEC documentation."

In order to get candidates excited, especially if they're Tiptoers or just starting to look, all of this needs to be combined into a career-oriented message. It will even get Explorers excited, although you'll have to push it to them directly, typically via an email. This type of story-based advertising opens your opportunity to everyone who is looking for a career move rather than just those who have an economic need to change jobs. It expands your target audience from 8% of the total fully-employed pool to 72%.

Job Branding vs. Employer Branding

There is so much being written about how to create an employer brand that I'll forgo any deep discussion on the topic. While an employer brand is important for attracting younger people in volume, especially recent college grads, it becomes less important for targeting the best people with more than 4-5 years of experience. If they're really topnotch, these people are looking for career opportunities. Many of these positions are with more nimble or fast-growing companies, including start-ups. In some cases a big employer brand can be considered negative from this perspective. Job branding bridges this gap.

Even if you don't have a well-known and positive employer brand, you can gain the same benefit by demonstrating that your open job has a direct impact on the ultimate success of the company. The EVP captures some of this by describing what the new hire can learn, do, and become if successful in the job. The sample Controller ad and the VP HR email below are good examples of job branding, tying the job directly to an important company initiative. Stating that the person in this role will be leading the product design for the new furniture line built via 3-D printing, or helping line managers better understand the financial reporting system, is more personally meaningful than selling the company brand via the same boilerplate information used on every other job posting. Going on to state how these initiatives will impact company success reinforces the job branding idea. For someone on the help desk team, job branding can start by stating that the position represents the true voice of the company. And then go on to say that every day this person ensures our customers get all of the technical support needed to maximize their product satisfaction and increase their personal connection to the company.

You don't need the big brass employer brand to attract the best people. Personalized job branding can have a far bigger impact. It must be included in your job postings and emails. Equally important, it must be customized for each job. Those with the big employer brands often get caught in this trap: overdoing the brand while ignoring how top people make career decisions. In the case of job branding, one size doesn't fit all.

Reverse Engineer Your Job Posting Process

Getting candidates to find your postings on the day they start looking for a job offers a significant hiring advantage, since there are no other companies interested in these candidates yet. These are the Searchers shown in the Early-bird Sourcing graph and pie chart above.

One simple way to see how well you're doing on the visibility of your job posting is to go to Google and type in what a typical candidate might search for when starting to look. You should also do this on the job aggregators, Indeed and SimplyHired. The idea is to see whether your posting is easily found using common search terms. If you don't have a well-known employer brand, it's even more important to be on the first results page and stand out with a clever title and a compelling first line. To gain a sense of this, here are the search results for a typical listing generated by this sample search: "accounting manager jobs near Irvine CA."

TYPICAL SEARCH RESULTS ARE FAR FROM IDEAL

Google | accounting manager jobs irvine CA

Web   Images   Maps   Shopping   More ▾   Search tools

About 204,000 results (0.29 seconds)

Ads related to **accounting manager jobs irvine CA** ⓘ
Accounting Jobs in Irvine - Info.com
www.info.com/AccountingJobsInIrvine
Get **Accounting Jobs in Irvine** Info Access 10 Search Engines At Once.

Accounting Jobs in Irvine - TheLadders.com
www.theladders.com/
Where Top **Accounting** Professionals Find Their Next Job. Join Now!
786 people +1'd or follow TheLadders

Accounting Manager Jobs - efinancialcareers.com
www.efinancialcareers.com/
Connect Directly to the Finance Job For You. Advance Your Career Today.

Accounting Manager Jobs - Irvine, CA | Simply Hired
www.simplyhired.com/.../jobs/...accounting+manager/i-irvine,...
Jobs 1 - 10 of 4583 – Every **Accounting Manager** job in Irvine, CA on the web. 4583
jobs available. Recent Jobs: Dell Quest Software **Accounting Manager** II, ...

Accounting Manager Jobs, Employment in Irvine, CA | Indeed.com
www.indeed.com/q-Accounting-Manager-l-Irvine,-CA-jobs.ht...
Jobs 1 - 10 of 901 – Find all 901 **Accounting Manager jobs** in Irvine, CA. Research
Accounting Manager salaries and view employer reviews in Irvine, CA.

Account Manager Jobs, Employment in Irvine, CA | Indeed.com
www.indeed.com/q-Account-Manager-l-Irvine,-CA-jobs.html
Jobs 1 - 10 of 1855 – **Manager** IPA Family Take control of your fiscal future! IPA
Family is looking for enthusiastic, entrepreneurial individuals to join its Insurance ...

National Account Manager Jobs, Employment in Irvine, CA | Indeed ...
www.indeed.com/q-National-Account-Manager-l-Irvine,-CA-j...
Jobs 1 - 10 of 241 – The Xerox **Account Manager** is a full-time position who expands
and retains customer base through account... sales and service on account ...

Accounting Manager jobs in Irvine, California | Monster.com
jobs.monster.com › ... › Accounting Manager › California
Jobs 1 - 10 of 10 – Explore **Irvine, California Accounting Manager jobs** and career
resources on Monster. Find all the information you need to land a Accounting ...

You Need to Be Found and You Need to Stand Out

Notice the actual search results from the first page only. On the
complete search, there wasn't a single company listed on the first five
pages of the search. All were job boards, search firms, or job aggregators. However, there were plenty of companies listed once I clicked on
these initial listings. So if you can't get on the top of the organic Google

search you'd better be at the top of the Monster, CareerBuilder, Indeed, or SimplyHired listings instead, at least if you expect to get people to apply for your openings when they just start looking.

Reengineer Your Application Process by Doing the Two-Step

Here's one macro process change that you should implement immediately if you get too many unqualified people applying to your job postings after making the advertising improvements suggested above. I call it the Two-Step. Here's how it works. Instead of pushing people into your apply process after seeing your posting, automatically email them back with another request. In the email state that your process involves more than just submitting a resume. If the person is interested in being an applicant he/she must submit a short write-up of some accomplishment most-related to your actual job needs. You should lead off this email with some complimentary phrase ("I'm impressed with your background"), and then describe the job in compelling terms before requesting the extra write-up. Alternatively, you could put the request for the write-up in the job posting itself, or in the email as shown in the VP HR sample email that follows. There are no compliance problems associated with this process. By default, most companies assume that once you post a job there is a legal requirement that the candidate must formally apply. There isn't. Consult your legal advisor for more specifics on this, but first read the general legal validation by David Goldstein of Littler Mendelson in the Appendix to understand why the Two-Step is an effective process for attracting more top people and screening out those who are unqualified.

The Two-Step will allow you to quickly sort out the robot responses and focus on only people who are truly interested in your opening. This will be about 10-15% of those who initially applied. Most people will self-select themselves out this way. More important, the accomplishment offered as validation will determine whether the person is a reasonable fit for the job. Not only is the Two-Step a great time savings, it also automatically brings the best people to the top of the list.

Don't Make Excuses, Legal or Otherwise, About Why You Can't Post Compelling Ads

Despite the obvious benefit to preparing more compelling job postings, the HR or recruiting department often makes the excuse that the company's legal department won't allow them. Don't fall into this trap. It is very important to recognize that these types of postings are in full legal compliance with U.S. labor law. The key for compliance (See the general legal validation overview in the Appendix) is that objective criteria be used to screen out unqualified candidates. In fact, one could contend that the ability to achieve SMARTe performance objectives is far more objective than having X or Y years of experience and a degree from some prestigious university or technical brilliance in some arena. Rarely are these factors scientifically determined by some type of job analysis. The one caveat that should be considered is that to be in full compliance all candidates for the same job opening need to be screened against the same standard.

Another point on compliance: nowhere will you find in any government pronouncement that your job postings need to be boring, nor do they need to be fully replicated copies of your internal documents required for getting your job requisitions internally approved. Somehow these became the de facto standard when job boards developed their first templates. This concept was developed and marketed based on the idea of giving companies the ability to easily post their job descriptions without much additional effort. Unfortunately, achieving economies of scale by posting internal job descriptions also drove many of the best people away because they wanted to be treated as individuals, not replaceable parts. This is a perfect example of unintended consequences, and the lack of a well thought-out talent acquisition strategy driving the process.

Some recruiters are initially reluctant to post these types of career-focused ads. Sometimes it's hard to do, since their systems are designed to only regurgitate the original job description. This is a terrible system design equivalent to giving the responsibility for hiring the best talent possible to the IT department. I like and use LinkedIn for posting jobs since it provides more flexibility on how these can be written. The short solution for everyone: add a compelling tag line to the title, expand the "Responsibilities" section to include the 2-3 most important performance objectives, and add a short task for the most critical skills, e.g., "use your 3-5 years in die casting manufacturing to rebuild our high-volume production line."

Some recruiters contend that passive candidates never see these ads, so posting them is unnecessary. I find this short-sighted. For one thing, I always send all my candidates a link to the posting to make sure they see it for themselves. This is a great way to get top people excited about what you're offering. This alone can often turn-around a reluctant candidate, or get a referral. Hiring managers and everyone on the interviewing team should take a look at the posting, too, to make sure everyone is on the same page regarding what's been publicly stated about the job.

Your postings do matter. They describe your culture and the importance of bringing strong talent into your company. Passive candidates will look at the actual posting before getting too serious. The ad is confirmation that the job behind it is worthy of serious consideration. It's also an easy way to create some instant buzz. Case in point: I sent the sample controller ad to CPA partners at the Big Four public accounting firms in the area. I had three referrals from these partners, and one partner told me he was going to use a version of the ad to help one of his clients find some other accountants. In addition, the finalists for the job all found the ad to be an important part of creating interest and convincing their friends and family the position was one worthy of serious consideration.

The Second 20 – Pushing Your Compelling Job Via Email to a Target Audience

The 20/20/60 Sourcing Plan is designed to ensure you're finding and attracting as many top active and passive candidates as possible. The objective of the first phase of the plan is to attract the attention of the best people as soon as they enter the job-hunting market. These are obviously active candidates. The second phase of the plan is designed to identify fully-qualified passive candidates who aren't looking for another job, but are willing to evaluate your opportunity. To attract their attention you'll either need to call, text, or send an email to them. Generating the list of names is the first step, typically using some type of Google search, getting referrals, or using LinkedIn Recruiter's searching tools. The job boards and job aggregators have similar search tools to search through their resume databases. These databases are full of active and passive candidates, so they're a good place to start looking. In fact, many of them have upgraded their searching capabilities allowing you to quickly develop a target list of reasonable prospects. Getting the right list of names is the initial challenge. Being clever using whatever search tools are available can help you separate the best from the rest. This will dramatically increase your productivity and yield (2-3X!) as you reach out to the right candidates with appropriate and compelling messages.

The Basics of Boolean and Some Clever Twists

Since every search starts on Google, LinkedIn or by digging into some database of resumes, knowing Boolean is essential. There are only five basic Boolean operators you need to master, and if you're not comfortable using them yet, it won't take too long to become proficient using just the information below. However, the real fun starts by adding some clever terms and twists that will allow you to narrow your search to only the best people within a specific specialty or demographic group.

The Only Important Boolean Operators You Need to Know

AND, OR, NOT or a minus sign, "_____" and (_____)

Rather than make too big a deal about this, view the summary of how Google uses these terms (http://budurl.com/EGclever). Most recruiters and sourcers use these operators with keyword terms to search through resume databases. Here's an example of a search string using these operators for Ruby software developers in the Irvine, CA area.

Type this string into Google and see what happens: (resume OR CV) -jobs -indeed -simplyhired -opening "Ruby on Rails" developers Irvine CA

All of the minus signs were used to minimize the number of non-resumes that were returned in the search. Without "NOT" or the minus sign equivalent term, more job postings than resumes for Ruby developers would have been retrieved. In this search more than 30,000 documents were returned in the search results. Without the NOT term there were more than one million!

Use Clever Terms to Narrow Your Search to the Best Prospects

30,000 resumes is obviously too many to work with, but this is just the first step and where being clever becomes important. Start by adding some Achiever terms to the search. For example, just by including the Boolean phrase "(award OR honors)" into the same Ruby developer string the list is narrowed down to 2,800 documents, one tenth as many. Reviewing just a few of the resumes you'll find other related terms to narrow the search even further. Some typical terms shown on the actual resumes returned included "Best in Class" award, "honors for design...", and "award for outstanding achievement." These are all people who have been formally recognized for doing superior work. This is a good group to start looking at in more depth. You can be also be more specific by function. For example, if you're looking for engineers restricting profiles to those with "(patent OR whitepaper OR speaker)" will return people who have been formally recognized for doing something important. When combined with skills "(skill1 AND skill2)" you can then find people who have been recognized for outstanding performance in a narrower area of expertise.

There are any number of generic Achiever terms you can use to build your search strings, plus every function has their own specific terms including academic honor societies. The term "(fellowship OR work-study)" will return people who have attended advanced company-sponsored education programs. The Boolean phrase "(club OR quota OR 100%)" will return sales reps who have been recognized for hitting their revenue targets. The term "Beta Gamma Sigma" will return people who have been awarded membership in the national business honorary society. From a practical standpoint you need to narrow the search to 100-200 resumes. Once you have your basic list using the Achiever and job function terms you can narrow it down further by job level, or to meet gender and diversity hiring objectives.

If you just want non-management developers you can reduce the size of the pool by adding the terms "-manager -Vice -VP -director" to the search string. For gender specific searches you could add "(she OR her OR woman OR women)" into the string. This works particularly well on LinkedIn profiles since the recommendations below the person's information is also searched, e.g., "She did a great job." An alternative for adding more women into your candidate pool would be using the Boolean phrase "NOT (he OR him OR his)," since these pronouns would be excluded in the search results.

To find candidates to meet diversity hiring goals you can add the obvious terms "Black" or "Hispanic" to the basic Boolean string. Also add the specific names of the Historically Black Colleges and Universities (http://budurl.com/EGhbcu) if your hiring needs are in a specific geographic area, for example, Howard University in Washington, D.C., and Morehouse in Atlanta. I recently found some top-notch engineers who were members of the National Society of Black Engineers (http://budurl.com/EBnsbe) this way. Since the founder of the National Society of Hispanic MBAs (http://budurl.com/EGnshmba) was a candidate of mine for a search many years ago, I often search on this group term whenever I need to find bilingual candidates. Even the term "bilingual" will help on this type of search.

Being clever using basic Boolean search terms is all you need to do to narrow your search to strong candidates with specific backgrounds in targeted geographic areas. Developing these terms is one of the primary reasons you should prepare an "ideal" candidate persona before starting any new search. Another big benefit: using this type of recognition term searching with a tool like eGrabber (http://budurl.com/AGegrab) allows you to quickly extract the email addresses from the documents without even looking at the resumes. You can then merge this email address file with a compelling email and within hours push your job opening to some very strong prospects.

You don't have enough time to work with everyone. Instead, restrict your sourcing efforts to finding and attracting the top performers in a specific niche job class. Rather than weeding out the weak, start with the idea of attracting the best. This will not only dramatically boost your productivity and shorten time-to-fill but also increase candidate quality. This is a pretty dramatic benefit just by being clever at Boolean.

Compelling Emails Can Be Pushed to Your Ideal Candidates Moments after Starting a Search

Emails are a great way to instantly convert your jobs into careers and demonstrate your culture. Following is an email similar to one I used two years ago to attract passive candidates for a VP Human Resources search we were conducting. It's written as a personal email from the hiring manager, in this case the CEO of the company. The original target list was generated using LinkedIn, and the email was sent within hours of starting the search. I started getting great responses the next day.

Whether you personally like the content of the email or not is not the issue. The issue is if your ideal candidate found it compelling and would respond. In this case, the email worked. I had calls from around the country who wanted to work for the CEO who weren't even in HR. Job postings and emails are designed to attract more ideal candidates. Most often recruiters put the wrong spin on their posting, trying to appeal to their own sense of style, rather than that of the person they're trying to attract. Regardless, as you read the email, why do you think it worked? Then think if you could you use the marketing ideas embedded in the email to attract more top people for your open positions.

PERSONALIZE YOUR EMAILS TO MAXIMIZE YOUR RESPONSE RATE

From	Lou Adler
To	jane@doe.com
	Add Cc Add Bcc
Subject	An open letter from the CEO to my next VP HR
	Attach a file Insert: Invitation Canned responses ▾

B *I* <u>U</u> T · ₸T · A · T · ☺ 🖼 ∞ ⌸ ⌸ ⌸ ⌸ ❝ ▤ ▤ ▤ *Iₓ*   Check Spelling ▾
« Plain Text

Jane,

I need help making our business become as big as it possibly can be. But, we can't do it without you.

Here's some background. Our company is growing very rapidly, and we've stretched our current HR policies, procedures and talent acquisition programs to the breaking point. We need to become totally focused on what really matters - every single person in this company and everyone we'll be hiring in the future. If we get this part right, there's no stopping us. To pull it off though, we need a top-notch VP HR and to build the right type of HR organization and infrastructure to address this unusual global opportunity. Without the right HR executive, we will not be successful.

Equally important, I need a strong HR business partner to help guide us through this exciting period in our company's growth. Not only will you have a seat at the strategic table, you'll often be at the head of it.

If you're up for the challenge, and this is something you'd like to consider, send me a half-page write-up of something you've accomplished that you think could make front page news. One of our board members will get back to you in 24 hours for an exploratory discussion. I'm looking forward to meeting you, and having you part of our dynamic team.

Emphasize Year One and Beyond, Minimize the Skills and "Must Haves"

At a minimum, add some creative taglines to your job titles. These alone will capture more attention, first because they're longer, and second because they're unusual. Here are some examples that actually worked in attracting more top people, without changing anything else. Not only are these interesting, they captured the ideal candidate's intrinsic motivator in 100 characters or less.

Flight Nurses – Helping Save Lives Every Day. The hospital chain couldn't find enough nurses to support their Medi-vac program after running a traditional ad for three months. This one change to the title resulted in 14 great prospects the first week, and six hires in three weeks.

Marketing Interns – Prepare Whitepapers in Any Color You Want. This well-known consumer products company couldn't compete in its local high-tech market for the best college students until it ran this ad.

Accounting Manager – Use Your CPA and See the World. This one converted heavy international travel into a career opportunity.

OGSKS – aka, Optics Geeks Seeking Kindred Spirits. This was for a government engineering position working on drones in a competitive high-tech market that had a terrible commute. The response was the highest this niche optics job board ever had for any engineering job.

Summary: Marketing works, and good marketing works better.

The Big 60 – Networking, Networking, Networking

While generating a list of names and sending compelling emails is relatively easy, in my opinion there's an even simpler and more important way to find great candidates. It's via picking up the phone, networking, and getting warm pre-qualified referrals. I consider this the super sweet spot for sourcing top candidates and why Virtual Talent Communities will become the new silver bullet for sourcing. To ensure you're finding and hiring the best talent available, it's obvious you need to be targeting the 40% of people who have classified themselves as Explorers and the 28% classified as Super Passives. Even if they're not personally interested in what you have to offer, the networking opportunities they offer can be invaluable, especially when Quality of Hire is the primary metric of success. That's why I believe 60% of any company's sourcing efforts should be on networking, networking, and more networking.

Build a Virtual Talent Community – The Sourcing Sweet Spot

Simply stated, a Virtual Talent Community (VTC) is the sum total of your connections' connections. This is especially important if you work for a large company, since it's easy to connect with any co-worker you don't already know. With LinkedIn Recruiter you can then search on their connections. This is a huge opportunity for finding great talent quickly, that most recruiters don't yet fully appreciate. A VTC implemented properly is how you build a dynamic, just-in-time, and proprietary network of passive candidates. Since it's constantly updated it's far superior to talent pipelines and resume databases. Getting all of your company's employees to proactively connect with their best former co-workers is how you can quickly expand your VTC and take full advantage of LinkedIn. Tapping into this VTC and getting referrals is the key to converting these connections from just names into hot prospects, great candidates, and ultimately superb hires.

> *G**etting all of your company's employees to proactively connect with their best former co-workers is how you can quickly expand your VTC and take full advantage of LinkedIn.***

The reason I like LinkedIn Recruiter is that it allows you to search on your connections' connections, rather than having to call someone and ask for referrals. This is a huge productivity gain. Here's how this is done. Start the hunt for some great prospects by searching on your co-workers' connections using the clever Boolean techniques described above. Then call the appropriate co-workers and ask them to qualify these people. When you call the prospects they will likely call you back if you mention the referrer's name. Of course, you'll only be calling people who you already know are qualified. This is a huge double-win that moves the search hiring process from a game of probabilities to one designed to maximize Quality of Hire right out of the starting gate. Too often, Quality of Hire is dependent on luck and timing. A

VTC allows a company to not only implement a Raising the Talent Bar program, but also measure and achieve it.

To get a sense of the impact of a VTC, visualize a network of people as more than just a flat list of names. It's the connections among these names that are the most valuable parts of the network. This is shown in the diagram. The direction of the connections is also important: In-Out vs. Out-In.

In-Out vs. Out-In Networking

Networking Starts by Finding People Who Are Connected to Your "Ideal" Candidate

Consider the dots in the center of the clusters as your connections. These people might have some strong people in their network – the cluster of dots around your connections – but it's unlikely you'll be able to connect with them by chance. Some proactive action on the part of a recruiter or researcher is required. An In-Out network is based on the concept that with LinkedIn Recruiter you can now search on these connections and ask about specific people. An Out-In network is based on the concept that a random active candidate will find someone they know in your company and attempt to get a referral. For job hunters this is a good idea, but for a recruiter trying to maximize Quality of Hire and time-to-fill, it's time consuming and success is problematic.

While the idea of using networks is growing, most companies are emphasizing the Out-In concept, hoping a good person who is looking finds one of your employees to connect with and uses the person to get referred into your company. This will happen now and then, but it's a very inefficient process that leaves too much to chance. I certainly wouldn't recommend building a talent strategy totally around this Out-In concept. However, building a talent strategy around an In-Out concept is another matter entirely. This is why I believe a VTC has game-changer possibilities.

In-Out vs. Out-In Networking

In-Out: a recruiter searches on a co-worker's connection, finds a few potential prospects, then qualifies these people and obtains a warm-lead

Out-In: a candidate finds a person in a company who knows the hiring manager or the recruiter who posted the job.

The big idea around a VTC is to leverage your employee referral program by getting your employees to proactively connect with their best previous co-workers. PERP is the term I use to describe this type of program – Proactive Employee Referral Program. Most people don't make it a point to connect with every great person they've ever worked with. Most connections are usually based on happenstance and convenience. Ensuring your company's current employees connect with these great people is the first step in building a robust VTC.

Find Well-connected Nodes to Launch Your Proactive Employee Referral Program

Finding which co-workers you want to connect with to obtain warm, pre-qualified leads is one of the key steps involved in preparing the candidate persona. As part of figuring this out, go beyond peer connections. Consider people who would have worked with your "ideal prospect" in a team or multi-functional-related business activity. These non-peer connections are referred to as nodes. Nodes are people who have worked with your target candidate in some capacity, and are more likely to give you a more honest appraisal of their ability than a true peer might. You'll also be able to expand the number of possible connections with nodes. When developing the target list of nodes, start by considering members of multifunctional teams the person would likely have worked on. For instance, product marketing people work with engineers, operations, legal and accounting. Also consider vendors, customers, consultants, possible mentors and mentees, and subordinate and supervisor relationships, including project managers. For example, if you're looking for software developers you should include Scrum project managers or product managers in your search for nodes. For accountants, you might want to consider financial executives and CPAs who still have strong connections to their public accounting firm alumni list. To find good sales people, you might want to find people in procurement who are dealing with sales people every day.

The point of this is to consider In-Out networking as a primary and more direct means to build your initial pool of prospects. This is how you tap into your company's ever-growing VTC and find prospects within a few days of starting any new search project.

Use the Cherry-Picking Technique to Quickly Obtain Warm Leads of Highly Qualified People

There are a number of critical strategic and practical advantages for creating a company-sponsored VTC built through proactive networking. First, you'll be able to very quickly get more pre-qualified referrals from your co-workers. This gives you a realistic chance to build a list of 3-5 prospects in 72 hours. (Remember, a prospect is someone who is perfectly qualified for the job and open to have a serious, but exploratory, conversation with the hiring manager.) Of course, you do need to be a good recruiter and networker to get any value from this process. After connecting with the referral you'll then need to present your opportunity and convince the person your opening represents a strong career move. While this part is time consuming, if you can get great referrals quickly through your VTC you've eliminated most of the up-front "getting the right names" drudgery.

To start tapping into your VTC, find some strong potential prospects by searching on your connections' connections. You'll be using the same "clever Boolean" techniques described earlier to do this. Once you have a few names ask your direct connection to qualify these people. This is what I mean by Cherry-Picking – picking only the best in the bunch to begin your networking process. This technique is much more productive than asking the same person, "Who do you know who's qualified?" Most of the time they'll only consider people they know who are looking – the Searchers or Tiptoers – not the people you've pre-chosen to present to them to ask about and qualify. Most of these will be true passive candidates – the 68% of the target candidate market you wouldn't have been able to find through traditional approaches. Since warm referrals will more likely call you back and are already pre-qualified, your productivity will soar along with candidate quality.

This In-Out networking process is not restricted to just your current employees – any well-connected person, i.e., node, will do. As an example, project managers are great nodes, since they work with all types of people inside and outside the company. However, leveraging your employee referral program is a great place to start, since most companies haven't begun to take full advantage of the current social media and networking tools now available. Regardless, whether it's a current employee or an external node, the key is to find people who would have personally worked with your "ideal" candidate in the past, connect with them, and then Cherry-Pick their connections. This forced recommendation process is a great direct means to develop a short target list of prospects in just a few days.

The Basics of First Contact Recruiting and Networking

> *R ushing too fast and selling lateral trans-fers mixed with hyperbole will close the door faster than you can remove your foot.*

Once you have a short list of pre-qualified names you'll need to personally contact these people, obtain their interest and further qualify them for your open position. My company offers an eight-hour training class (http://budurl.com/aghub2) on how to do this. Here's the 15-minute version:

1) **Ask yes questions.** When you get someone on the phone, ask if they'd be interested in talking for a few minutes about your position if it represented a significant career opportunity. Be vague about the job, since you might be able to modify the job somewhat for the right person. Too many recruiters start off describing the job, which is a sure way to stop the conversation if there's no instant interest. In this case you've not only lost a future prospect, but also a current networking opportunity.

2) **Review the person's profile before describing the job.** If the candidate is willing to discuss a possible career opportunity, don't launch into a sales pitch about your job opening. Instead spend a few minutes reviewing the person's LinkedIn profile. As you're doing this, look for areas where your opening might represent a possible career move. Consider things like the scope and focus of the job, the size of the team and budget, and the importance of the position and its impact. If you've prepared the performance profile and recruitment marketing material, especially the EVP, as suggested earlier, you'll have enough

information to craft a statement about the career merits of your opportunity.

3) **Bridge the Gap.** Most candidates – especially those who aren't looking – normally ask about Day 1 criteria when first contacted by a recruiter – the job title, company, location and compensation. This information is what they use to decide if they should spend any more than a few minutes discussing the open job to see whether it's in the ballpark, career-wise. Recruiters then typically fall into an unsuspecting trap by giving them the answers. Recruiters incorrectly or naively assume that by telling them this information they'll be able to quickly screen out the apparently uninterested or unqualified. Don't succumb to this Day 1 "give me the info" conversation trap! As soon as you hear these types of questions make sure the warning bells are ringing loud and clear. This will help you overcome the natural tendency to talk about Day 1, and instead shift the conversation towards Year 1 and Beyond criteria. While there are many ways to do this, one way is to walk the person through the hiring timeline introduced in Chapter One describing the difference between Day 1 and Year 1 and Beyond decision-making. Start this by saying, "If the job doesn't represent a good career move, the compensation really doesn't matter. So let's first see if the job is worth a more serious discussion, and then we'll get into the compensation and related issues." This is a great way to quickly regain control of the conversation.

4) **Don't sell the job, sell the next step.** When dealing with passive candidates, it's best not to move too fast. Too many recruiters operate in a transactional mode, attempting to fill a position with the next best person contacted. This approach won't work with a person who's interested in a career move. In order for the person to have enough information to consider the job a potential career opportunity you need to move in graduated steps. This allows the person to gather more and more Year 1 and Beyond information in order to fully appreciate the significance of the position. Hiring managers need to be part of

this information-sharing process and be totally open to talk to prospects on an exploratory basis. A series of small steps like this is what it takes to convert a "no" into a "maybe," and a "maybe" into a "yes." Rushing too fast and selling lateral transfers mixed with hyperbole will close the door faster than you can remove your foot.

5) **Build a 10-minute relationship by controlling the conversation.** Don't let prospects opt out before they have a full understanding of your opportunity. This is a critical point. By controlling the conversation around Year 1 and Beyond, and getting the candidate to describe his or her background first, the recruiter can then figure out if the job represents a career opportunity or not. It takes at least 10 minutes for both the recruiter and the prospect to share enough information for both to feel comfortable about moving on to a more serious in-depth discussion, if warranted. The recruiter must not rush the process, nor let the candidate rush it, either. Then, even if the person isn't ideal or interested, you'll at least be able to network with the person. You need to invest at least 10 minutes to build a worthwhile networking relationship. Don't short-circuit it. It will prove costly to both the recruiter and the prospect.

As said in the opening to these last two chapters, this isn't everything about sourcing, but it's probably all you'll need. Too many people are in a constant chase for the next sourcing silver bullet, overlooking the fact that some great tools already exist to find anyone. You just have to put a 20/20/60 Sourcing Plan in place and then implement it properly.

CANDIDATE ADVICE
Do the Unexpected to Find More Jobs!

If you're now looking for a job, or are considering it, there were some great tips in this chapter. All you need to do is reverse engineer how companies find candidates and before you know it, you'll have a few more interviews lined up. Here's my quick list to get you started:

Forget resumes, build an online presence instead. I'm going to suggest minimizing the need for a formal resume because a LinkedIn profile accomplishes much of the same. It's even better, since it's always current. Most companies are okay with using LinkedIn profiles, at least for the first step. Regardless, prepare a basic resume in case you need it, and have it with you at all times, but don't overdo it. Caveat: make sure your resume is consistent with your LinkedIn profile. The real point here is that your online web presence should be representative of who you are as a potential new hire. First you need to determine whether you can be found on Google or LinkedIn by searching your name and some brief keywords, like company, academics, job title, and specific honors and awards. If you can be found this way, does your profile describe what you want a potential new employer to see and discover? (See below on how to be found without your name.) Your online presence should include a link not only to your LinkedIn profile but also your blogs, postings, Pinterest board if you have one, and Facebook page, if it's public. Collectively, all of this represents you, and the more visible it is, the better the chance someone will find you. If the profile is strong, someone will give you a call. In fact, if it's really strong, someone will call you before you even start looking. Being found by an Early-bird recruiter is a great place to be. It's always best to make career decisions when you're not desperate.

Be Known. One way to improve your online presence is to participate in groups, blogs and discussions. The idea behind this is to become known as a subject matter expert in some field. Recruiters hang out in these groups and look for people who answer the toughest questions and provide the most relevant information. One major component of the Achiever Pattern is coaching and advising peers and being recognized by them for this effort. It might take some time to build up your online presence and credibility, but it's well worth it. For one thing, recruiters will seek you out and contact you to determine whether you're interested in a new potential opportunity. For another, they'll check you out this way to see how active you are and what you say. This is a great way to establish your credibility as well as increase your visibility.

Give yourself a 30-second onceover. Have someone look at your resume or LinkedIn profile for only 30 seconds. Then have them tell you what stood out. You want to make sure that your most important information stands out in a quick review. Recruiters decide in about 30 seconds if it's worth reviewing any profile in more depth. What should stand out are your titles and company names, including the first three lines of your LinkedIn profile. The second line is your personal branding statement and you must get this part perfect. From this they'll get a sense of who you are and your career progression. If this is positive, they'll then look for your academic background and get a sense of your total years of experience and the focus of your most recent work experience. They'll also be on the lookout for negatives as part of the first 30 seconds (e.g., too much turnover, lack of progression, too much irrelevant information, etc.). If everything is positive with no big negatives, they'll spend another minute or two digging deeper to see if it's worth contacting you. You have 30 seconds to have your profile speak for you – make sure it shouts what it needs to say.

Add recognition terms to your resume and LinkedIn profile. Put a list together of every award and honor you've ever received. Put the big ones under some type of award or honor heading. Getting recognized by others for doing outstanding work adds credibility to your profile. Read the chapter describing how to identify the Achiever Pattern when reviewing a person's LinkedIn profile or resume. Make sure you modify your profile accordingly, at least to the degree possible. Recommendations and endorsements are part of this, but not a big part, so don't overdo this unless they're very credible and support the basic profile. If you've held leadership positions in some outside groups, these are worth adding, but consider any possible downside. There are some activities that people might consider ill-advised or inappropriate. Regardless, remember that you're trying to use your profile to demonstrate that you're a person who's in the top 25% in your specialty. So emphasize this and make sure it's clear and obvious for someone who's only going to give your profile an initial 30-second review.

Be found. Go to Google and use the "clever Boolean" ideas mentioned earlier for searching for resumes and see if you can find yourself. First try this out with standard keywords. You do need an online resume posted on a major site like CareerBuilder, SimplyHired, Indeed or an alumni site, since many recruiters hunt through these databases to find candidates. If you're not easily found, look at the resumes that are there and see if there are some patterns that exist that bring some people to the top of the search. Add a section with appropriate keywords to the bottom of your resume to make sure that you're not inadvertently filtered out. (See Rick Gillis' book "Job!" for more on this important topic.) To get more exposure, redo your resume by benchmarking the best ones you find, and then make sure yours is posted on the more common sites.

Proactively network with your best previous co-workers. From a company perspective, the way to find candidates quickly is to create a Virtual Talent Community. Your job as a candidate is to become part of as many of these as you can. Then when a job is opened some recruiter will be able to find you when they conduct a search on their co-workers' connections. Of course, once you're found, you need to stand out during the 30-second LinkedIn profile review. That's why all of the ideas mentioned above must be done. What I've just described is In-Out searching: starting with a job and getting pushed to the company's employees' connections.

This is what recruiters are starting to do, so make it easier for them and yourself. You can view this In-Out process as an employee referral program on steroids. While this process might not get you noticed right away, it might be how you will be contacted in the future.

Tap into your existing network via LinkedIn. Connecting with your best previous co-workers also works from an Out-In standpoint, and if you're looking for a job, this might be a more direct route for getting an interview. Here's how: if you find a posting on LinkedIn or Facebook, you'll frequently see a list of people who are most directly connected to the person who posted the job. You can then contact the person you know to find out more and possibly get an interview. If you don't see the list of names, go to LinkedIn and see if you know someone in the company already who can connect you to the hiring manager or department head. (Try to avoid HR if you can, since it will slow the process down.) This approach works very well if the person you're contacting can vouch for your capability. It becomes a nuisance call if the connection is very casual. That's why it's important to cultivate these connections. Of course, at the core, you need to deliver on every assignment you've ever had so the person you're requesting help from can confidently vouch for you.

Nurture some nodes. One of about half-a-dozen ways good recruiters use to find candidates is to obtain high-quality referrals from nodes. A node is a person who has worked closely with the potential candidate in some capacity other than a direct peer. Some examples of nodes would be partners at CPA firms who know financial executives and their own firm's alumni, buyers who know sales people, project managers who have led large multi-functional teams, and lawyers who have put together business development deals. This is just a start of a full list, but the idea here is that the best recruiters connect with these nodes to get referrals. If you want to be one of the people being referred you need to be directly connected with well-networked people. Reverse engineering the process for a candidate suggests that they connect with and nurture these same people. Start with nodes you know who can vouch for you and then work their network with them to find other potential nodes. When you contact these people continue to get referrals. If you keep the network growing this way, someone will soon hear about a potential job opening you'd be interested it. Do this backwards, too, by finding jobs that are appealing and then find some people in your network of nodes who are directly connected in some way to the company in your sights. This takes some effort, but a LinkedIn JobSeeker premium account ($10/month) is a great bargain and will help you find and manage the connections.

CANDIDATE ADVICE
Don't Apply to Ads

Applying to an ad should be the last thing you should do. The probability of getting a job this way is pretty low. Instead you need to do whatever you can to network yourself into an interview before you push the "Apply" or "Send Your Resume" button. So before you resort to the least-effective way to get an interview, here's my suggested sequence of things you should do before applying to a job posting:

• Find someone you know at the company who can vouch for your ability.

• Find someone you know at the company who can at least recommend you to the hiring manager.

• Find out who the hiring manager is or the hiring manager's boss and send the person a link to your LinkedIn profile. Add something that is distinctive and helpful. This could be how you'd address the needs of the actual job, an unusual way of viewing the job or problem, or a link to a relevant article or blog post. The idea behind this is to ask for a 10-minute phone discussion. Don't move too fast. If you get the online meeting you'll need to use this to get an onsite interview or a formal online interview.

• Talk to someone in another department who might work with the person in the role. For example, a product marketing person probably works with engineers and engineering managers, or someone in finance. By connecting with someone in these one-off functions and engaging with them, they might be willing to recommend you as someone who understands multi-functional problems.

• Find some other external nodes who have a vested interest in getting the job filled with someone they know. For example, CPA partners want their alumni in important corporate accounting positions. A vendor might want a production engineer to help develop product specs for a new automated line.

Be different. Here is a great article on using Pinterest.com (http://budurl.com/pinresumes) as a means to create a unique, graphical resume by being creative, being different, and being memorable. I'd even go so far as to say to be creative in a way that demonstrates strengths and talents. For example: marketing people need to demonstrate their marketing expertise not only in their resume design but also how they get their profiles distributed; visual designers of any type need to present their resumes in such a way that demonstrates their design skills; bilingual people need to show their resume in all of their languages; and engineers somehow need to present their technical ability graphically, visually, and mathematically. You no longer need to be restricted to the format of LinkedIn, Facebook, or the standard resume to present yourself. Use your imagination and talent, and present yourself in a way that's unique to you. This is part of the 30-second rule and online presence points made earlier. Being different doesn't just apply to formatting the resume. It's how you get noticed, it's how you write emails, it's who you connect with, and it's who you are. I had a web designer apply for a job by presenting a detailed analysis of every page of my client's interactive web site. The quality and depth of the analysis got him an instant interview. Some caveats go along with this "being different" idea: don't be offensive, don't use bad taste, temper being weird, and don't be boring unless that's part of the job.

Build and nurture the network. A very talented woman – the daughter of a neighbor – has networking aced. She's progressed very rapidly in marketing in the entertainment industry by building, nurturing, and using her network. I understand she attends 2-3 networking meetings a month. As a result, she never has to look for a job; someone is always reaching out to her. Like I tell hiring managers and recruiters, if you're reacting to a hiring need, it's too late. Under a short-term business need to fill the position you'll always make a compromise. The same is true for managing your career. If you're always reacting or forced to find a new job, you'll always make a compromise. Finding a new great job or finding a top person to fill an open slot should always be done before you need the job or person. This is why proactive networking is so important. LinkedIn provides the platform to do this. Use it wisely. Go through every job-hunting idea presented so far in this book. Assign a proactive or reactive label to each one. Then work them all until you've got them nailed. Emphasize the proactive ones when you're not looking. You'll know if you have networking done right when you hear about jobs before you start looking, or when you find that a few perfect opportunities just happen to be available after contacting the best nodes in your network.

Summary – Sourcing Tools and Techniques

- **Implement a 20/20/60 Sourcing Plan.** In order to attract the best active and passive candidates you should split your sourcing efforts into three categories. Twenty percent of your time should be on preparing compelling ads that can be found. Another twenty percent should be spent on sending targeted emails to people identified via searching for resumes and LinkedIn profiles. The other sixty percent should be focused on networking, obtaining pre-qualified warm leads and contacting these people.

- **Reverse Engineer Your Job Posting.** Conduct a search wherever you've posted your job using terms most candidates would use to see if it can be found. Don't include your company name. If your ad can't be found on the first page or two, you have some work to do to get it there.

- **Post compelling ads, not internal job descriptions.** There is no law or logical reason to post your internal job descriptions for candidates to see. Instead, tell compelling stories emphasizing the Employee Value Proposition (EVP), highlighting critical job activities, and describing just a few of the big skill requirements somewhere at the bottom.

- **Do the Two-Step to minimize unqualified candidates.** If you get too many resumes just ask everyone to submit a write-up of something they've accomplished that's most comparable to the primary objective on the performance profile. This is perfectly legal.

- **Job Brand your postings.** Even if you have a great employer brand, tie your job to a major company project or initiative. You must do this if you don't have the big brand to attract people. Working on something meaningful and important is a critical aspect of job satisfaction. It's also a great way to excite candidates and demonstrate to them that their work is important to the company's success.

- **Use "clever Boolean" to target high achievers for your niche target market.** You don't need to be overly technical to obtain great search results. But you do need to know the basics of Boolean, and you do need to be clever. Add appropriate achiever and demographic terms to the basic Boolean operators in order to build an instant talent pipeline. Then email them a compelling career-oriented message.

- **Build a Virtual Talent Community (VTC).** PERPing your ERP is how you can build a robust VTC in months. (ERP: employee referral program. P: proactive.) This will become the sourcing silver bullet of the future. Your co-workers' connections should be the first step in any passive candidate sourcing efforts. Since you can search on these connections using LinkedIn Recruiter you should proactively ask the people at your company to begin connecting with all of their most-qualified previous co-workers.

- **Use the Cherry-Picking technique to obtain pre-qualified warm referrals.** By searching on your connections' connections using LinkedIn Recruiter you can ask your direct connections about the best people you find. Since these people will more likely call you back, and you already know they're strong prospects, your productivity will soar in comparison to making cold calls.

- **Become a great networker.** Calling passive candidates requires strong recruiting skills. The recruiter must control the conversation and prevent people from opting out until they fully understand the career merits of your job. At a minimum, you'll be able to connect with these people on LinkedIn and search on their connections.

- **Candidate's View: become someone worth contacting, then be sure you're found.** Give your resume and LinkedIn profile a complete overhaul. You want the 30-second review to shout, "Contact me!" To get to this point, you also need to ensure recruiters can find you. So do what recruiters do and find some people just like you. Then do what they did to get to the top of the search listing.

- **Candidate's View: second, spend more time networking rather than applying.** Work on building a network of people who can vouch for you if their company is looking for people. Networking is already a more efficient way to find a job than applying directly. It will be even more important in the future.

Chapter 9

Recruiting & Closing
Top Candidates

Hiring a top person is not just about interviewing, it also requires strong recruiting and negotiating skills. If the person is top-notch and in high demand, he or she will likely receive a counter-offer or an offer from a competing organization. Too many managers, and most recruiters, think recruiting is mostly selling and wooing, using hyperbole, extra compensation, and multiple levels of pressure to seal the deal.

In my mind, this is exactly the wrong way to recruit a top person. The key is to ensure the candidate clearly sees the job at hand as the best career opportunity among competing alternatives. If the package is competitive, even if it's not the best comp-wise, then closing the deal should be focused on having the candidate understand the short- and long-term value of each opportunity. Much of this can all be accomplished using the two-question performance-based interview process described in this book. When candidates know they've been evaluated properly and in comparison to real job needs, they consider the subsequent advice provided by the recruiter as more meaningful.

Recruiting starts by conducting an in-depth professional interview. The fact that the company has high selection standards sends an important message to the candidate: the organization is focused on hiring the best. On a more micro level, using the interview to seek out differences in what the candidate has accomplished in comparison to the performance profile is a powerful means to demonstrate the actual career opportunity you're offering. I call the sum of all of these differences the "opportunity gap." These differences could include the size of the project or team, the importance of the work, the opportunity for accelerated growth, and what the candidate can learn, do, and become. Collectively, these gaps can represent a significant career move for the candidate. If big enough they can more than offset the need for a significant compensation increase.

Too many managers expect candidates to accept lateral moves. This is unlikely when dealing with a top-person with multiple opportunities. It's also unwise when hiring anyone, even if they don't have other options. Hiring a person based on an economic need is unlikely to inspire the person to work at peak levels, especially once the economic need is met. In my opinion, it's better to offer a person an incentive to grow, a chance to maximize their abilities, and to become better at what they want to do. This way, the person views the new job as a worthwhile career move, not as just a means to a paycheck. With this "opportunity gap" underpinning, negotiating the offer then involves a tradeoff between career growth, opportunity, and the compensation package. Providing someone with a chance to become 10-20% better, or more, is a great way to increase job satisfaction, motivation, and on-the-job performance. The tradeoff might be a little less in Day 1 compensation.

While the Performance-based Hiring process is an easy-to-use and practical way to assess a candidate and set up the recruiting process, it offers the following less-obvious benefits:

1) Ensures that the best performer is hired, not the best interviewer.

2) Demonstrates that the job has a big impact on the company and that the company is not just trying to fill a position.

3) Gets high-demand candidates excited enough about the opportunity that the person will not only sell you on why they're worthy, but they'll later sell their family members, friends, co-workers, and personal advisors as to why your job is the best among all competing alternatives.

4) Minimizes the threat of counter-offers and competitive offers where money becomes the biggest factor in the candidate's decision.

Little of this can be achieved without a performance profile to make the comparison and the use of the two-question performance-based interview to obtain the information. Here are some ideas on how to achieve these multi-level objectives during the interviewing and assessment process.

Stay the buyer from beginning to end

If a candidate has an economic or career need for your job, it's pretty easy to stay the buyer. Needy candidates are always in sales mode, trying to convince you they're worthy. However, any high-demand candidate who has multiple suitors is a different person entirely. In this case, managers and recruiters switch roles and go into sales mode, using hyperbole and PR-speak in an attempt to convince the hot prospect of the worthiness of their offer. Even if the person doesn't opt out under the pressure, it ends up in a bidding war if you decide to make the person an offer. Staying the buyer not only prevents the problem, but also increases assessment accuracy, while minimizing the need to pay compensation premiums.

Here's how staying the buyer works. Start by listening 4X more than you talk. Asking tough, detailed questions about the person's accomplishments is the easiest way to do this. This is what the Most Significant Accomplishment question is all about. If you preface the question with a description of what you need accomplished and why it's important to the company, the best and most worthy candidates will naturally get excited and try to convince you they're qualified. This is called the pull-toward interviewing technique, using the actual job to get the candidate excited about what you're offering. During the interview, don't accept superficial answers. Peel the onion and get facts and specific details about the accomplishments. Challenge the person. Top people will leave this type of interview knowing they've been assessed properly, and if the job appears to be a real career move, thinking about why they want it, not why they don't.

Make the candidate earn the job; it has more value this way. This is how you stay the buyer, by making the candidate become the seller. As a result, they'll go home telling their family, friends, co-workers, and advisors why the job represents a great career, despite a modest compensation bump. The key to remember here is that if candidates can't sell themselves on the merits of the job, they won't be able to convince anyone else, either. Since top candidates never make the decision to switch jobs alone, this is a critical step you must address in the recruiting process.

Create the career gap. In order for a job to represent a career move it needs to offer both stretch and growth. Stretch represents the actual difference between the person's current job and the job you're offering. It covers the scope and scale of the job in terms of team size, overall responsibility, budget, what the person can learn, and the challenges involved and their impact and importance to the company. A more important job in a smaller company represents stretch from an impact standpoint. Growth is the future. It represents what the person can become if the job is handled successfully. This relates to taking on bigger assignments with more significance, promotional and unique learning opportunities, and getting exposed to more challenging situations. While hard to quantify, a job 15-20% bigger than the person now holds would represent an excellent career move. If the combination of stretch and growth is less than 10%, the job is more a lateral transfer, and if more than 25%, the job is most likely too big a jump. As part of demonstrating this type of opportunity, have the candidate meet other people who have been successful and have taken on bigger roles in the company. You need to prove the company's claims of growth opportunities; otherwise you're pulling a ruse that will lead to disappointment, underperformance, and turnover.

The two-question performance-based interview process can be used to help both the interviewer and the candidate figure out the size of this opportunity gap. First, use the most significant accomplishment question to compare the candidate's accomplishments to the performance objectives listed in the performance profile. The differences represent the opportunity gap. Then use a push-away as part of the follow-up questions to get the candidate to "own" it. One way to do this is to state your concern about the size of the gap (e.g., team size or company pace) and then ask the candidate to describe something he or she has accomplished that's most comparable. Good candidates will not be deterred or offended if the assessment is accurate. Instead, they'll try to convince you (i.e., sell you) as to why they're qualified. Some candidates might be overly concerned by the size of the challenge. This is one way to have candidates self-select themselves out of the job. Strong candidates will likely want to better understand the challenge involved and ask a series of appropriate follow-up questions. Expect this. Be concerned if the questions are not forthcoming or not relevant. You can force this type of questioning dialogue by using the Problem-solving Question.

By challenging or pushing away the candidate, the person understands clearly why the job represents a possible growth opportunity. A bunch of small gaps like this can often represent a big career move. For example, a slightly bigger team, more influence, bigger impact and broader responsibility combined with a faster growing company, is often all you need to convert what seems like a lateral transfer into a significant career opportunity. A performance-based interview achieves this far better than overt selling. If an offer is made, the candidate is then in a better position to favorably compare your opportunity among others from a long-term growth perspective, rather than strictly on the size of the short-term compensation increase.

Minimize the negatives; accentuate the positives. While Year 1 and Beyond criteria represents the bulk of why top people select one offer over another, minimizing the candidate's current company frustrations is often an unstated component. Leaving a bad boss, doing work that's stifling, sacrificing quality for expediency, or not being respected or heard are common reasons why fully-employed people begin looking for new opportunities. As you begin the phone screen, ask the person why he or she is looking for a new job, and what the person would need in a new job if they were to switch companies. Then ask them why this issue is personally important to them. Getting the answer to "Why is this important to you?" will get at some of the person's underlying frustrations. If you can minimize these problems, you'll increase your odds that you'll be able to hire the person on reasonable terms.

Don't make an offer until you're 100% sure it will be accepted. This is a critical aspect of closing, and why preparing a performance profile at the beginning is so important. For a top person, especially a passive candidate, taking a new job represents a critical personal decision, one that affects family, friends, and close associates. These decisions are not made quickly or lightly. Too often, companies hurry the process to fill an opening. This clash of needs often precludes either party from making the best decision. By moving as fast as possible, but not faster than the prospect is able to digest and consider everything, you can achieve an optimum balance.

But don't wait until you're finished interviewing to make an offer. By then too many things are left uncovered and the unexpected "surprise" is always around the corner. Upon getting the offer, the typical candidate response is then, "I'll have to think about it," an outright "No," or entering into some type of competitive bidding process with the deepest pockets winning the rights to the candidate. This converts the negotiating process into a series of reactions and counter-reactions. You won't have to endure this if you test every aspect of the offer before it's made, and then don't make the offer formal until the candidate is 100% committed to accept it.

Testing and Negotiating the Offer by Getting Continuous Concessions

Don't wait until the end of the interviewing process to negotiate the offer. Instead, start right after the phone screen. Here's how this is done. First, you need to stay the buyer throughout the process and create the career opportunity gap as described above. Second, lengthen your interviewing process to add an exploratory step at the beginning and add one or two additional steps during the assessment. A second round of interviews including a problem-solving take-home question should be part of this expanded assessment. Regardless of what you add, the key is to not allow the candidate to proceed to a subsequent step without getting some type of concession. For example, if you're a recruiter suggest that while the candidate is a bit light in comparison to the other candidates being considered, you'd like to present the candidate to the hiring manager as a high-potential person worthy of serious consideration. However, since the candidate's compensation is already at the high end of the range, going forward would mean any potential salary increase would need to be modest. Don't proceed unless the candidate agrees to this concession.

After the first round of interviews, ask the candidate how your job compares to others the candidate is considering. Use the candidate decision matrix below to guide your questioning. Ask if the person considers your opening as one of their top one or two possibilities. If the candidate is excited about moving to the next step, obtain another concession. This could simply be a discussion around your benefits package if it's a bit weak, or your company's vacation policy. The point here is by discussing all of the points of a possible offer before it's extended, no one will be surprised about the terms when one is actually made. Often you'll need to prove more long-term growth as a tradeoff for some real short-term problem or concern. This is where the decision matrix can be helpful in demonstrating this.

If the candidate does not consider your job as one of their best opportunities, find out the person's concerns. Ask that if these could be addressed adequately or modified somewhat would the candidate be willing to then go forward in the process to become a finalist. If not, there is something else unspoken preventing the candidate from proceeding. Persist and find out the problem. You might not be able to overcome it, but at least you'll know why. This technique is called "closing upon a concern." It's important to use this technique to uncover and address all concerns the candidate has before you make a final offer.

While you want to test all of the specific components of an offer before it's formally made, you also want to test your candidate's interest at every step. Early in the process it's just asking if the person would be willing to move to the next step if it could be arranged. Don't automatically say, "We'd like to arrange a second round of interviews, are you interested in proceeding?" This hands control to the candidate. This is a big no-no. The recruiter needs to control the conversation. If the candidate agrees to the conditional "if it could be arranged" statement, you can determine the candidate's true interest and address any concerns and gain a small concession. As you progress in the process, you can ask when the person could start if an acceptable offer was made. It's a great sign if the person provides a start date. If not, you'll have to find out their concerns and see if they can be addressed.

As you finalize the offer package, ask the person when he or she would formally accept it if an offer was made in a few days. An "I have to think about it" type of response is not good. Testing done properly would result in a response like, "Right away, once I read it over thoroughly." You do want the candidate to fully understand every aspect of your offer before accepting it, but this can be done by testing and negotiating every point ahead of time. If the candidate requires more than 24 hours to make a final decision once an offer is made, there's a problem. Typically, testing as described was not done properly or there was a rush to close. Here's an important rule to follow: don't extend the formal offer if the candidate requires more than 24 hours to accept it. Of course, this won't work for college grads or if there are some legal or contractual aspects to consider, but testing will still uncover most concerns and lead to a smooth closing process.

Here's an important rule to follow: don't extend the formal offer if the candidate requires more than 24 hours to accept it.

While there's more to negotiating the offer, if testing is done properly, by the end of the process all aspects of the offer will have been tested and agreed upon before it's officially presented. Equally important, by delaying the process this way, the candidate is fully aware of the career opportunity you're offering and has discussed it thoroughly with everyone. This process allows the candidate to fully evaluate all of the long- and short-term factors involved in making a critical career decision and comparing yours to competing offers or a potential counter-offer.

The Candidate Career Decision Matrix

We suggest providing the candidate a formal decision-making form in order to fully understand your opportunity and to compare other career options. This is shown below (a full version is included in the Appendix). While the form is somewhat overwhelming at first, it's useful for everyone (candidates and his/her advisors, recruiters, and hiring managers) to understand what's at stake when comparing opportunities and changing jobs. The form itself allows a person to compare different jobs based on short- and long-term criteria. It also offers a guide to consider compensation from a strategic and tactical perspective. The overall idea is that in the long run, career growth will have a far greater impact on compensation than getting a big bump when changing jobs. If you're the recruiter or hiring manager you need to prove that your opening is in fact a career move, not a lateral transfer.

CONSIDER EVERYTHING IN BALANCE TO
MAKE THE RIGHT CAREER DECISION

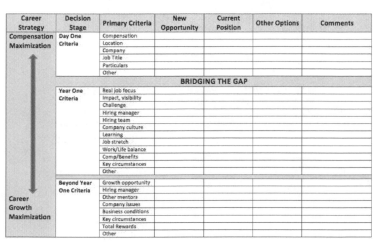

Career Strategy	Decision Stage	Primary Criteria	New Opportunity	Current Position	Other Options	Comments
Compensation Maximization	Day One Criteria	Compensation				
		Location				
		Company				
		Job Title				
		Particulars				
		Other				
		BRIDGING THE GAP				
	Year One Criteria	Real job focus				
		Impact, visibility				
		Challenge				
		Hiring manager				
		Hiring team				
		Company culture				
		Learning				
		Job stretch				
		Work/Life balance				
		Comp/Benefits				
		Key circumstances				
		Other				
	Beyond Year One Criteria	Growth opportunity				
		Hiring manager				
		Other mentors				
Career Growth Maximization		Company issues				
		Business conditions				
		Key circumstances				
		Total Rewards				
		Other				

Don't compromise your long-term growth
for short-term convenience

The career decision matrix is comprised of these four core elements:

1) **Decision Stage.** This is shown in the second column breaking
the decision criteria into three big categories: Day 1, Year 1, and
Beyond Year 1. This corresponds to the Time-phased Hiring
and Decision-making Process chart first presented in Chapter
1, showing how hiring mistakes occur upon first contact by
emphasizing Day 1 criteria over Year 1 and Beyond. In the table
the typical criteria a candidate uses to make a decision is listed.
I suggest giving the candidate a short list of these criteria early
in the process. Then let the candidate add his/her other consid-
erations and put the list in priority order. As a recruiter I then
guide the candidate at this stage, suggesting that balance across
all of the time factors is important. Too often candidates overvalue the short-term over the long-term, so this is an important

discussion. If you're a candidate you should prepare this decision list for yourself. The idea is that career growth will get you where you want to grow and go, not the comp you're paid, security, or location.

2) **Compensation and Career Strategy (the first column).** Trading off compensation in the short-term for long-term opportunity is discussed in more depth in the following candidate-facing chapter. The quick take on this is to suggest that maximizing compensation is a short-term career strategy that emphasizes Day 1 criteria over Year 1 and Beyond. Companies are largely at fault by overvaluing skills and experiences for screening and selection purposes, in essence, treating jobs as commodities. As a result, compensation becomes the big differentiator and a bidding war erupts for the best candidates. By preparing performance profiles and emphasizing Year 1 and Beyond, compensation is naturally considered in balance as part of a whole package. A career maximizing strategy is one where the Day 1 compensation is fair, but the big rewards are based on successful performance of the job: Year 1 and Beyond.

3) **Comparing the Opportunities.** Candidates, hiring managers, and recruiters alike need to use this section to help understand how the opportunities available compare to others the person is likely to have. Often these are not obvious, especially if compensation differences or relocation loom large in the candidate's decision. The basic idea is to ensure the candidate has full information to make a proper career decision with the long-term career opportunities having more value than the short-term criteria. Sometimes the job can be enlarged to improve the opportunity, so don't exclude any job or any person if there's a reasonable fit. Using this form for guidance and keeping an open mind, and after a full set of interviews, the candidate will likely have more information about your opportunity than other opportunities being considered. On this basis, if your job is the best from a long-term career standpoint it should be the one selected assuming a reasonable Day 1 compensation package.

Candidates should seek out this information before making any yes/no decision, including receiving a huge counter-offer. Often short-term data is overvalued when long-term decisions need to be made. This can become especially disastrous when it comes to changing jobs. In this case, everything should be fully considered in equal balance across all opportunities.

4) **Bridging the Gap.** Too many candidates, especially passive candidates who are initially contacted by a recruiter, ask the classic Day 1 series of questions: what's the money, what's the job, where is it located, and who's the company. Based on this, they decide to engage in a more detailed conversation about the job to learn more, or decide to pass. This is a big mistake if you're the candidate. If you're the recruiter don't let your prospects opt out at this point. Candidates, don't opt out either even if the recruiter allows you to. The big idea behind this is that candidates should evaluate Day 1 criteria after learning about Year 1 and Beyond. Everyone needs to fight the kneejerk reaction of focusing on, and overvaluing, Day 1. Just consider how many career opportunities were lost as a result of this superficial decision-making approach. For one thing, jobs are often modified to meet a top person's needs. For another, compensation is always negotiable, so what's described up-front is a crude filter at best. Third, the long term is more important from a career standpoint than the short term. Fourth, both candidate and recruiter alike lose the opportunity to network. Even if the job isn't a great fit, there might be another one around the corner, or you might be able to suggest someone who finds the opportunity a great career move. Play it safe, not quickly, by bridging the Day 1 thinking gap, and find out what's behind the opening conversation.

Recruiters can use this career decision matrix to advise the candidate every step of the way. Allow the candidate to personalize and prioritize the factors when comparing competing opportunities, but offer advice if some of the shorter-term factors are weighed too heavily.

By testing each aspect of the offer before making it formally, you're in a position to ensure the candidate has all of the information needed to fully evaluate your opportunity in comparison to everything else being considered. While you want candidates to think about your offer, you'll know exactly what the person is thinking if you don't rush to make it. Once you make a formal offer candidates are less open. Often this is because the candidate has other opportunities and doesn't want to be pushed by a recruiter. Without a formal offer in hand, the candidate is much more revealing in expressing concerns. For example, if the salary is less competitive the candidate can use your offer to negotiate something better with someone else. However, by testing the salary, the candidate will tell you whether it's adequate or not. You can test every component of an offer this way without getting into a reactive bidding war. Being the last company to make a formal offer has obvious advantages, including increasing the likelihood your offer will be accepted.

Hiring the best people, especially passive candidates, requires much more than an accurate interview. It's also much more than reactively moving into a hyper-sales mode to convince a hot person of the merits of your job opening. Done properly, it's an end-to-end process starting with a clear understanding of real job needs and the use of an in-depth interview that's been integrated with a professional recruiting process that also maps to the decision-making process of top professionals. The two-question Performance-based Hiring interview and recruiting process was designed to meet these exacting requirements. As you'll discover, if you haven't already, this is why it works so well in all types of hiring and recruiting situations. The career decision-making matrix can help you guide the process along. While you won't hire every candidate using it, both you and the candidate will at least know why.

CANDIDATE ADVICE
On Negotiating and Accepting Offers

Negotiating an offer is not about maximizing the compensation – it's about ensuring you're getting the best career opportunity possible. In my mind as long as you're receiving a competitive compensation package, you'll maximize your compensation in the long term by advancing more rapidly than you would otherwise. To better understand my thinking here, it's important to understand the difference between a career growth maximization strategy and a compensation maximization strategy.

A career growth maximization strategy is based on the concept that high visibility, rapid growth, and learning lead to bigger jobs and more rapid promotions. Significant compensation increases follow growth rather than lead it. A compensation maximization strategy is based on the idea that a person needs to make sure each move results in a major compensation increase. This can backfire very quickly, since the person is expected to perform at peak levels right away.

Candidates beware! A lot of bad things can happen when a short-term compensation maximization strategy is used to make long-term career decisions. A comp max approach typically puts the new hire into the upper levels of a salary range, leaving little room for future salary movement, even for doing good work. This is frustrating. Worse, higher salary levels lead to higher expectations of performance, and when not met, the person is considered underperforming. Since the person is "overpaid" given his or her experience level, the person is unlikely to meet the elevated job expectations, and even less likely to exceed them. This leads to a cascading negative effect and deep frustrations for both the new hire and the hiring manager. This is how a comp max strategy can quickly lead to career stall and a plateau.

Candidate career advisory! A lot of good things can happen when a growth maximization strategy is used to compare and select one of several competing job opportunities. For one, by entering in the middle to lower end of a salary band, job expectations are somewhat lowered, so it's easier to beat them. For another, the hiring manager will recognize your value system as more performance-driven than compensation-driven. A good rule of thumb here is that there is more upside potential when you're underpaid for the work you're doing than being overpaid for it. When you're talking with a recruiter or hiring manager, focus more on the challenges, visibility, and impact the person in the job can make, not the compensation package. This will take care of itself if you're successful.

A good rule of thumb here is that there is more upside potential when you're underpaid for the work you're doing than being overpaid for it.

Managers and business executives tend to be more open-minded with people who are willing to prove their worth rather than having to be paid in advance for it. This psychological aspect alone offers a huge benefit to those who pursue a growth max career strategy. There's much less strain in negotiating the offer, and much more tolerance on the part of the hiring manager if things go awry. In my opinion the short-term gain in compensation is not worth the long-term costs of fighting for a maximum increase. Instead, suggest you'd rather have a fair offer coupled with a short-term review, with any compensation adjustment based on how well you perform.

Top people innately know that progressing rapidly is the key to maximizing compensation. Average performers tend to focus on maximizing compensation in the short term while ignoring the long-term costs and negativity involved. The point: think like a top person, and you'll more likely become one.

Summary – Recruiting and Closing

- **Start recruiting right away.** Don't wait until the end of the interviewing process to begin recruiting the candidate. By then it's too late. It takes multiple meetings for a person to fully appreciate the career merits of the job. If they're significant these career growth factors become more important in accepting an offer than short-term external factors like compensation, location, title, and the company name and brand.

- **Stay the buyer.** Candidates might balk at this, but the recruiter's role is to ensure the person has all of the information necessary to make a reasoned career decision. By staying the buyer, candidates are forced to sell themselves if the job represents a career move. Selling too soon cheapens the job and shifts the focus to the wrong factors.

- **Use the interview to create the career gap.** The difference between the candidate's actual accomplishments and the performance objectives listed in the performance profile represent the growth opportunity inherent in the job. Candidates will only fully appreciate this if they've been interviewed thoroughly using the performance-based approach recommended in this book.

- **Test the offer before it's formalized.** Make sure you cover all aspects of the offer by asking the candidate if he or she would accept it as described. As part of this ask when they could start, when they'd give formal notice, when they'd give you verbal acceptance of the offer, and when they would actually officially sign the offer letter. Do all of this before giving them the formal offer. If they balk on any item, stop and find out why.

- **Force the candidate to make a formal evaluation of your offer.** When considering and comparing offers, most candidates overvalue the short-term compensation package. Less effort is spent on evaluating the long-term career value of an offer. The offer evaluation form highlights the key factors needed to make a balanced long vs. short-term assessment in comparison with all other opportunities. If you're a recruiter or hiring manager, make sure your candidate gets the information needed to make a proper evaluation. If you're a candidate, it's more important that you seek this information out.

- **The candidate view – pursue a career growth maximization strategy.** When you're negotiating an offer, don't push for the biggest financial package. Be reasonable. Instead, push for a job that gives you the biggest chance to demonstrate your full ability. Being slightly underpaid is not a bad thing if it leads to significant career growth. Significant career growth is how you maximize your compensation.

Chapter 10

Job-Hunting and Interviewing for Candidates

Throughout this book, there have been notes, comments, tips, and ideas on how to handle the job-hunting and interviewing process. In this chapter, I'll tie all of this together and describe exactly what you must do to get ready for the all-important interview.

The Real Purpose of the Interview, and What It Isn't

None of what's been presented here so far should be a surprise to those of you who are looking for a job. Even if you're not looking for a job right now, it's worth reviewing this section. It will help you better understand the performance-based interview and recruiting process from the perspective of the candidate. If you're a recruiter you should review this with your candidates to help get them ready for the interview.

Big Note: the purpose of the performance-based interview is to measure a person's ability to meet all job needs. It's not to measure the person's presentation or interviewing skills. Getting a candidate prepared to accurately and effectively describe his/her comparable accomplishments is part of this. If the person's accomplishments are not comparable to what's needed to be done, then it's okay to eliminate the candidate from consideration. It's not okay to dismiss a person based on emotions, intuition, feelings, or a superficial or biased assessment. If you're a candidate it's your responsibility to make sure you're judged accurately and fairly. If you follow the tips and techniques described in this section and throughout the book, you'll improve your odds of being judged fairly. None of this will help you get a job you don't deserve.

Critical Steps to Get Ready for the Performance-based Interview

Here are the steps you must follow exactly as described in order to ace the performance-based interview. If you're a candidate you must own each step. They're described in detail below. If you're a recruiter, send a copy of this book to each of your candidates and make sure they are fully prepared for the interview. Go through each point with the candidate and make sure they're ready. It's far easier to prepare a worthy candidate to interview properly than look for another candidate. This addresses an extremely common hiring problem: interviewers misjudging a worthy person using flawed or superficial information.

CANDIDATE ADVICE
Preparing for the Interview Checklist

....

❑ **Be Prepared.** Don't wing the interview. Prepare as much as you would for any important management presentation.

❑ **Don't look at your resume during the interview.** Looking is a sign of nervousness, or fabrication. You need to know everything on the resume without hesitation.

❑ **Use the SAFW format to answer each question.** A complete 1-2 minute answer is the sweet spot for length and content.

❑ **Ask the interviewer to describe real job needs.** Force the interviewer to ask about relevant topics.

❑ **Focus on the opportunity, ignore the compensation.** Compensation increases will follow great performance.

❑ **Demonstrate interest and ask about next steps.** Get the interviewer to commit to something, and if he/she hesitates, find out why and respond.

❑ **Demonstrate how you develop solutions rather than giving the solution.** Most Problem-solving Questions are designed to understand how a person develops a solution, rather than the actual answer.

❑ **Ask relevant, rather than self-serving, questions.** Demonstrate that it's what you can do for the company, not what the company can do for you.

❑ **Practice, practice, practice.** Everyone gets a little nervous during the interview. To get through the initial two minutes of discomfort, practice getting nervous by answering questions to a friend or family member.

....

If you're a hiring manager, get ready for some good candidates who know how to present themselves properly. They will be evaluating you too. The best people expect to be thoroughly vetted. Don't let them down. It will be your loss.

As you read the following, recognize that the underlying premise of a Performance-based Interview is to find candidates who are motivated and competent to do the actual work required. All too often candidates are judged largely on their presentation skills and their raw technical competence. This is why the traditional one-on-one interview is such a poor predictor of on-the-job performance[4]. Worse, most interviews last less than one hour, and more times than not, only 30 minutes. Despite the superficiality of this, these interviewers get a full yes/no vote. As a candidate your job is to ensure you're measured on the right factors, whatever time is given to you. Consider also that the objective of the first interview is to get invited back for another round, not to get the job. Following the guidance below you'll put yourself in the best position to get both.

Be prepared.

There are a number of critical steps involved in getting ready for the interview. Some of these relate to self-preparation and being able to confidently present your capabilities during the interview. Others relate to thoroughly knowing the company you'll be interviewing with. As a minimum, have a list of your major accomplishments by job title and company already summarized with all of the details memorized. As part of being prepared, put together a list of all of your skills, traits, and personal attributes. Next to these traits, associate them to one of your major accomplishments and prepare a specific example for each trait. This way you'll be able to weave in your success traits when you describe some of your accomplishments. The example chosen provides the proof needed to the interviewer you actually possess the trait. Interviewers will use these examples to compare to the performance profile describing what the person hired for the job needs to do to be considered successful. This is the "F" for "few examples" in the SAFW method described below for framing and answering questions.

As part of your preparation, review the company's website, its financial performance, and the posted job description. Make sure you have some understanding of how the job relates to the company's business. Prepare specific questions that allow you to better understand the primary

---

4 Hunter and Schmidt. *The validity and utility of selection methods in personnel psychology: Practical and theoretical implications of 85 years of research findings.*

focus of the job, where it fits organizationally, and some of the key performance objectives. Some of these should relate to resource availability, time frames, company culture, and the hiring manager's leadership style. Also, be sure to review the LinkedIn profiles of everyone you'll be meeting, especially the hiring manager. This is invaluable information.

Don't look at your resume during the interview.

You must know your resume inside out, including every date, title, and company. Looking at a resume is a sign of lack of interest and/or preparation, or fabrication. Regardless of the cause, which is probably due to temporary nervousness or excitement, the interviewer will unconsciously think the worst. So have someone ask you about all of the details on your resume to help you prepare. If you're a passive candidate and truly not looking for a change, make sure you know your LinkedIn profile inside-out anyway. This is a sign of professionalism, showing respect to the interviewer.

Follow the SAFW two-minute response for each answer.

Your answers to most questions need to be 1-2 minutes long. If your answers are shorter or longer than this, you send a message that you're a poor communicator. SAFW is a way to format the answer – **Say A Few Words:** make an opening **S**tatement, **A**mplify it, add a **F**ew examples, then **W**rap it up. The most important part of this is the example. Prepare a relevant accomplishment for each of your key strengths. Obviously these accomplishments should relate to real jobs needs as much as possible; that's another reason why preparation upfront is so important, especially reviewing the job description. Practice using the SAFW answer format by having someone ask you to describe your most significant accomplishment. Then make sure you keep this to less than two minutes. Before you know it, all of your answers will be the correct length and appropriate for just about any question you're asked.

Ask the interviewer to describe real job needs.

Most interviewers won't be asking the right questions. Technical people will focus on your technical capability, HR will focus on team and cultural fit, most senior managers will judge you largely on how well you communicate and answer hypothetical "what if" questions. Regardless of the type of questions, ask the interviewer to describe real job needs, some of the associated challenges involved with the job, and why the position is being filled. You'll be able to address many of your subsequent responses based on this framework. More important, once you know exactly what the person in the role needs to do, you can describe some of your major comparable accomplishments. This approach ensures the candidate is being assessed properly focusing on real job needs, not some artificial standard or hidden biases. Here's a short blog post (http://budurl.com/LIace) I wrote for LinkedIn that provides more insight on how to do this properly.

Focus on the opportunity and ignore compensation.

Review the section on how recruiters should test offers and negotiate compensation multiple times. In the final analysis, lack of money is not nearly the problem everyone thinks it is. Unfortunately recruiters, managers, and candidates all use it as a screening tool. If an opportunity can accelerate your personal growth, great compensation increases will follow. For the right person, companies are willing to adjust their compensation ranges. Frequently jobs can be adjusted in scope and size to better suit the candidate's requirements. However, none of this adjusting is possible if money is used as an early filter. In this case, all it does is prevent further conversation. To prevent this from happening to you, and only when asked, make sure you clearly reflect the importance of the opportunity, stating the compensation will be on your list as only one factor in your decision, while an opportunity to make an impact will be at the top of the list. Under no circumstances ask the recruiter or whoever contacts you first, "What's the compensation?" It doesn't matter. You have much more negotiating power when you're the chosen one; you have none when the company starts looking for someone to choose. More important, don't ignore the idea that the recruiter might have other opportunities available or that the job could be scoped differently once you've had a discussion.

In the career planning and negotiating section of this book, I strongly suggest that a career maximization strategy will do more for growing your compensation than a compensation maximization strategy. Too many people try to max their compensation when changing jobs. This can backfire in a number of ways. For one thing, more is expected of the person, failure is not tolerated, and the honeymoon period is shorter. A person who asks for a fair compensation package, plus a chance to prove himself or herself, is always looked upon more favorably.

Demonstrate interest and ask about next steps.

At the end of the interview tell the manager that you're interested in the job, and you want to know what the next steps are. If the person hesitates, ask if the person believes your background is appropriate for the job. If not, find out where from a performance perspective you fall short. Then attempt to recover by describing an accomplishment that best meets the company's need. Most managers tip their hand if they're interested in the person being interviewed. Typically they describe the next step, they ask specifically about the person's interest in the job, or they try to convince the person that the job is worth serious consideration. If none of these clues are forthcoming, the candidate has a chance to reposition himself or herself by proactively seeking out reasons why the manager is not more positive. If you earlier asked about real job needs you'll probably know some of these shortcomings yourself. Fill in the gaps with another example of an accomplishment. If you didn't ask about the job, ask before the interview is over. Better late than never.

Demonstrate how you develop solutions rather than giving the solution.

Answering Problem-solving Questions are often challenging. The purpose of these is to assess job-related thinking skills. The answer to the questions is less important than how you arrive at the solution – at least it should be. So rather than give an exact answer, describe how you'd get to the answer and the process you'd use to achieve a solution. Asking clarifying questions and seeking external advice is part of how you would solve the problem, so demonstrate this during the interview.

There are two types of Problem-solving Questions: those that are relevant and meaningful, and everything else. Trick questions fall into the everything-else category. Reread the section on asking and answering the Problem-solving Question for more on this important topic. A relevant question is one that relates to actual problems the person taking the job is likely to encounter. For example, in sales this might be dealing with a difficult customer. In engineering it might be coming up with an idea to overcome a technical challenge. In accounting it might be understanding the meaning of some financial regulation and how to respond. The purpose of the question is to better understand how the candidate would approach resolving the issue. As part of your response ask questions to better understand the problem, the scope, and some of the parameters. The quality of your questions is a key part of what's being evaluated, so don't rush to a conclusion. Once you have framed the problem and provided a logical course of action to solve the problem, provide an example of something you've accomplished that's most comparable. This is referred to as the Anchor and Visualize pattern – demonstrating both your thinking and problem-solving skills, together with your ability to actually do the work required to implement a solution.

While these types of job-related Problem-solving Questions are very useful for assessing thinking skills, the use of trick questions is not. A classic trick question Microsoft used to ask in the '90s was "why is a manhole cover round?" A trick-question is an attempt to get at thinking skills, but since few are actually job-related, the answer provided can't be evaluated properly. It's left up to the interviewer to make the call, which is problematic at best. Lists of trick questions (http://budurl.com/agtrick) are published that you may find humorous, particularly, "How would you get an elephant into a refrigerator?" Funny or not, you will be judged on how you answer the question. Despite their uselessness, these are still pretty prevalent, so you need to understand how to handle them.

I tend to be direct and confident, so my approach might not be universal. I remember an early interview I had for a financial analyst position at the corporate office of a Fortune 50 company just after earning my MBA from UCLA. The interviewer asked me how to market light bulbs. I told the person I didn't have a clue, but I could tell him how to build a factory to make them, and how to determine the exact cost. He liked the answer, and I got the job, but I didn't think much of the person asking the question.

My advice for answering these types of questions is to ask questions to understand the person's objective. Then go through the process used to figure out the answer. Your problem-solving and thinking skills are what should be assessed and this approach will give you the best shot at answering it properly.

Ask relevant questions.

> *If the job doesn't represent a career move, you shouldn't take it under any circumstances.*

If the job doesn't represent a career move, you shouldn't take it under any circumstances. So when you get the chance, don't ask "Day 1" questions concerning the compensation or benefits. Instead first focus on the importance of the position and the impact it could have on company performance. Find out why the job is open, and ask about resources, reporting relationships, and the quality of the people already on the team. Especially ask about the hiring manager's leadership and coaching style. Fit with the hiring manager is the prime contributor of success or failure when taking a new job, so this needs to be a critical focus area for the candidate. The quality of your questions is a critical aspect of the assessment, so don't take this lightly. Do your homework, and make sure the questions are relevant. Make sure you ask some of these questions toward the end of the interview when you know some details about the job. This will have a double impact, since the questions can't be prepared. Lack of meaningful questions is a sign of lack of interest, incompetence, or that the candidate is just looking for a lateral transfer, not a career move. Don't ignore this principle:

> *Good people always ask good questions.*

Practice.

I suggest that a person should spend as much time preparing for the interview as they would for any important management presentation. Three to four hours is not unreasonable.

As a recruiter, I coach my candidates who are a little weak on interviewing by having them answer questions and provide appropriate examples. Part of this includes preparing the SAFW response for a few of their major accomplishments. I then ask them to answer these over the phone with me before the actual client interview. I push hard on the fact-finding to see how much the person has practiced. If not enough, I either cancel the interview with the hiring manager, or delay it. In my opinion, hiring is too important for anyone to wing it, whichever side of the desk you happen to be on. If you're working with a recruiter, practice your answering technique with him or her. If you're not working with a recruiter, practice with someone who will judge you harshly. Then when the actual interview arrives, you'll be in a position to ensure you're being assessed properly.

Overcoming temporary nervousness.

Assume you'll get nervous. In fact, practice getting nervous by having someone like a friend, a child, spouse, or significant other ask you a few serious questions. If you've practiced enough, the nervousness will pass quickly. One way to overcome temporary nervousness is to reverse the tables and ask the interviewer a question at the beginning of the interview. This puts the burden on the other person to answer, giving you a short pause to catch your breath and regain your composure.

A question like, "Could you give me a quick overview of the job?" early in the interview is a logical and appropriate question to ask. Some others include, "The recruiter indicated that (something) was important, but the posted job description said (something else). It would be helpful if you could clarify this," or, "Would you mind rephrasing the question slightly, so I could give you a more focused answer."

Of course, the questions need to be relevant and appropriate, but the idea of asking questions to help understand what's being asked is useful in all cases, and especially helpful if you're a bit nervous. Giving specific examples is another way to ensure your answers don't ramble. Frequently people who get nervous either talk too much or not enough. Neither one is good. Giving an example that best illustrates your point is a great way to relieve nerves and provide the interviewer with relevant information.

Improve your first impression.

It isn't as hard at it may seem to make a good first impression. Be clean, neat, respectful, friendly, and on time. Self-confidence can do wonders for all of this. That's why preparation as described throughout this book is so important. As described above, asking a few early and pertinent questions is also helpful; this shows you've prepared and are engaged.

In addition, having a normal conversation about "stuff" is a great ice-breaker, too. "That was a great game yesterday, wasn't it?" is much better than a short grunt and falling into the chair with a disinterested gaze. Shake hands firmly. Look the person in the eye when answering questions – don't stare – and answer the initial questions for about 30 seconds to a minute each. This will get you into the flow of the conversation. DON'T BE LATE. Being late is not a meaningful predictor of on-the-job performance, but interviewers actually make judgments based on this, assuming lack of motivation or interest. So don't be late, but call if something happens and you're going to be late. Don't be too early, though, but get to the location 30 minutes before the meeting and review the company website and job description again while you're waiting in the parking lot. Read about the company's latest news and weave this logically into the conversation if possible.

If your first impression is a true handicap, make sure you've been thoroughly phone-screened and vetted before the first face-to-face meeting. During the phone screen make sure you get a good understanding of the job and tell the interviewer about a relevant accomplishment. This should be the basis for getting the onsite interview. This knowledge will naturally reduce the impact of a less than a top-notch first impression, since the interviewer will quickly remember the real reason for inviting you was based on your performance. Don't dismiss this point about the preliminary phone screen. I have a personal rule to never meet a candidate face-to-face until I've conducted a thorough phone screen. This lets me be much more objective even if the person's first impression is not perfect. If you're a candidate who is not blessed with a great first impression, you must ask to be phone screened first. Just say you want to make sure your background fits with the company's needs. You should do this anyway, regardless of whether you make a great first impression or not. At a minimum, you'll save a lot time.

The Importance of Preparation

Let me repeat the importance of preparation:

Being totally prepared allows you to think about all of the other things going on in the interview without having to think about the answers to the questions.

If the interviewer is leaning forward, that's a good sign. Arms crossed, leaning back, or the interviewer glancing at his/her watch or cellphone is not.

Make sure you lean forward in the chair when responding. Ask if you could take a tour of some relevant area at the beginning of the interview if possible. For example, if you're interviewing for a maintenance supervisory role it would be important to see the maintenance area. You'll quickly observe some problems you'll be expected to solve. Being prepared allows you to control the events to some degree, ensuring that the interviewer has all of the information necessary to make the correct decision. You won't get invited back every time or get every offer, but being totally prepared will give you the best shot at both.

Too many good candidates don't get the opportunities they deserve due to lack of good interviewing skills. Thoroughly understanding the points raised in this chapter will help improve your odds. Even if you're not looking, don't ignore the call from the recruiter. Be open-minded. When talking with the recruiter don't focus on the short-term stuff like the job title, location, and compensation. Instead ask about the challenges involved in the job, the resources available, and the company's financial position. Provide high-quality referrals if you're not personally interested. Networking like this is critical in the era of social media and LinkedIn. Being prepared for the interview often starts long before you are seriously considering a job move.

I want to repeat that this book has been written to help companies find, assess, and hire fully qualified and motivated people. It's also been written to help these fully qualified and motivated people get the job they deserve. It was not written to help unqualified people get a job they don't deserve. Unfortunately, if you're a fully qualified person who isn't a great interviewer or doesn't make a great first impression, you will likely be judged unfairly. In this case, it's your responsibility to make sure the company assesses you properly. Following the advice in this chapter will help you level the playing field.

Summary – Performance-based Hiring from the Candidate's Perspective

- **Be prepared.** Don't wing the interview. Prepare as much as you would for any important management presentation.

- **Don't look at your resume during the interview.** Looking is a sign of nervousness, or fabrication. You need to know everything on the resume without hesitation.

- **Use the SAFW format to answer each question.** A complete 1-2 minute answer is the sweet spot for length and content. If your answers are much less than a minute, they will not be understood or remembered. If they're longer than three minutes the interviewer will think you're too self-absorbed, boring, or insensitive. The example chosen for proof is the most important part of your SAFW responses. This is what interviewers will remember and use to make their assessment.

- **Ask the interviewer to describe real job needs.** Force the interviewer to ask about relevant topics. Make sure you ask why the job is open, some of the big challenges and problems that need to be addressed, and areas that need to be improved or upgraded. Then give an SAFW response using your best and most comparable accomplishment as proof you're fully qualified.

- **Focus on the opportunity, ignore the compensation.**
  Compensation increases will follow great performance.
  A career maximization strategy will maximize your
  compensation in the long-term. A compensation maximization strategy will stunt your career growth in the
  long-term.

- **Demonstrate interest and ask about next steps.** Get
  the interviewer to commit to something, and if he/she
  hesitates, find out why and respond. The key is to find out
  why the interviewer thinks you're not fully qualified, and
  then provide a detailed example of your best comparable
  accomplishment.

- **Demonstrate how you develop solutions rather than
  giving the solution.** Most Problem-solving Questions are
  used to assess thinking and problem-solving skills. Rather
  than jumping to a conclusion and spouting out an answer,
  ask enough questions so you fully understand the problem. Then describe how you'd go about figuring out the
  problem and what you'd need to do to put a plan together
  for resolving it. Top this off with an anchor, describing
  something you've accomplished that's most comparable.

- **Ask relevant, rather than self-serving, questions.**
  Candidates are judged by the quality of the questions they
  ask. So choose what you ask wisely. Use these questions
  to first understand the challenges involved in the job and
  to then demonstrate that you're fully qualified to handle
  them. If the job doesn't represent a career move, it doesn't
  matter what the short-term benefits are. Within a few
  short months you'll be disappointed. Use questions to
  first clarify job expectations, and determine whether it's a
  job you can handle and one that represents a career move.

- **Be more prepared than everyone else if you don't make a great first impression or aren't a great interviewer or get nervous.** Do everything described in this chapter enough times so you can coach others on what they should do to get ready for the interview. If you can advise and coach others, and they find it useful, you're ready to be interviewed yourself.

Chapter 11

Implementing the Performance-based Hiring Talent Acquisition Strategy

Here's a simple diagram that summarizes why most companies can't hire top people on a consistent basis, and why even those that do work too hard at accomplishing it. The concept represented is that in order for any business process to work effectively – like hiring top talent – every aspect needs to be in alignment. For talent acquisition this includes the talent strategy, the supporting tactics and processes, and the people involved, primarily the hiring manager, the recruiter, and the candidate.

DON'T LET YOUR TACTICS AND PROCESSES DETERMINE YOUR STRATEGY

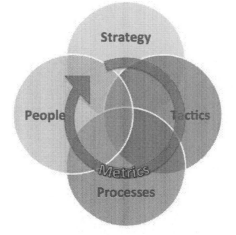

Use metrics to ensure your talent acquisition programs are in full alignment

Strategy needs to drive the process, and everything needs to follow suit. This is rarely the case as I point out in the Catch-22 video I prepared with LinkedIn (http://budurl.com/LICatch22). So if you don't want to enter the Staffing Spiral of Doom as described (FYI: it's a scary place to be), or want to get out of it quickly, you need to closely follow the advice presented in this final chapter. The key point of the video is that you can't use an ill-conceived and misaligned talent surplus strategy in a talent scarcity situation.

From a process control standpoint metrics are needed to make sure everything is in alignment with the overarching talent acquisition strategy. In the preceding diagram this is represented by the circular arrow. If the metrics are used for both process control and process improvement, the common overlap at the center of the four circles would continually get bigger as the four circles are drawn together. When the process is out of alignment, including people who are all using different decision-making tools, the overlapping common area decreases in size as the four circles become further apart. This represents an out-of-control and inefficient process. You can probably figure out for yourself what the situation is like at your company on this measure. Threading this narrow needle is a challenging task for a candidate, especially if you're looking for a career, not just another job. It's equally as hard for recruiters and hiring managers who want to hire great people, but are thwarted by their company's bureaucratic and ill-advised processes and procedures.

When the process is in alignment, however, the performance trifecta of maximum quality, shortest time-to-fill, and lowest cost is easily achievable. This book has been about what it takes to achieve this performance trifecta.

Hiring the Top 25% A-Z Review

In the opening chapter of this book I introduced the idea that bad timing decisions make a big difference on how jobs and people are evaluated. This is shown again in the diagram. The point of this was to suggest that managers and recruiters use inappropriate criteria to make critical hiring decisions, screening and filtering candidates on factors that don't predict success. Candidates are prone to similar problems emphasizing short-term compensation and convenience over long-term career growth. Under these conditions, it's rare when the best decision is made by anyone. The root cause of this is lack of proper alignment with strategy and decision-making on both sides of the desk.

HIRING RIGHT STARTS BY THINKING BACKWARDS

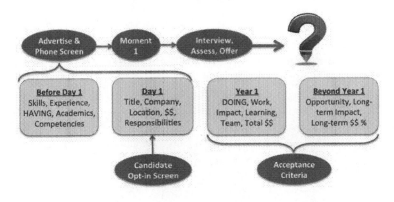

Attract, Recruit, Assess and Hire People Based on What They Need to Do and What They'll Become if Successful

For one thing, whether you're looking or hiring, there is too much focus on Before Day 1 and Day 1 criteria. Companies use these criteria to advertise for and screen candidates out and in. Most candidates overvalue Day 1 criteria when looking for a new job or when thinking about getting serious about an opportunity when called by a recruiter. Yet most people – especially passive candidates – decide to accept or reject an offer based on Year 1 and Beyond criteria. Interviewers all overvalue Moment 1 – based on the person's first impression – and then conduct some type of loosely structured assessment to determine who gets hired based on whether they initially liked the person or not. As a result of these mis-timings, it's unlikely the best person is seen or hired, and predicting the performance of the person ultimately hired is more luck than science. This book made the case that Performance-based Hiring could be used as the foundation for the hiring process that addresses most, if not all, of these problems. I'll use this final chapter to help you evaluate the process for yourself to see if the claims hold water in the real world of hiring.

On Becoming a Better Manager

In many ways this is not really a book about hiring. It's a book about becoming a better manager. This starts by hiring the right people. And hiring the right people starts by defining the work they need to do to be considered "right." This is why the performance profile is such a critical piece of the hiring puzzle. Gallup's Q12 (http://budurl.com/agq12) study first publicized in 1999 in the great business best-seller, First, Break All the Rules – What the World's Greatest Managers Do Differently, provided more than ample evidence that managers needed to understand real job needs if they wanted to maximize their team's performance and job satisfaction. Google's Project Oxygen (http://budurl.com/agoxygen) echoed the same theme: people want their managers to support and develop them while providing meaningful and important work.

My theme for this book for those doing the hiring is pretty basic: hire people who are motivated and competent to do the work you want done. Everything presented here is driven by this simple premise. The theme for those wanting to be hired, or thinking about taking another job, is equally as basic: only take jobs that offer the opportunity to become better at something you want to do. That's why everyone – recruiters, hiring managers, prospects, candidates, and interviewing team members – must focus on Year 1 and Beyond criteria, and overcome the powerful and insidious tendency to filter everything through the lens of Before Day 1, Day 1, and Moment 1.

Performance-based Hiring provides the foundation for all of this. As far as I'm concerned it represents the front-end of effective management: define the work you want done, and hire people who are capable and motivated to do it. If you're the hiring manager, during the interview tell your candidates what you need done and why this work is important. Then make sure they've done something comparable. It does not have to be, nor should it be, identical. Negotiate the offer based on why this work represents a career move for the person. Emphasize and prove that what you're offering is not a lateral transfer. Presented properly, a big compensation increase will then be less important. This only works if it's true, meaning the job offers lots of stretch and opportunity for growth coupled with a better set of circumstances, meaning it improves the candidate's situational fit factors: a better job, a more supportive manager, and/or a more conducive culture. Once on the job, collectively this will all drive motivation, performance, and job satisfaction. During the on-boarding period review the performance objectives in more detail. Make sure you and the new person are in agreement and put the tasks in priority order of importance.

Use an updated performance profile and the talent scorecard to develop and guide your new hire every step of the way throughout the first year. On a regular basis reevaluate the person using the talent scorecard and the 1-5 scale to see how well predicted performance maps to actual performance. Keep track of the differences and determine whether some of these could have been more accurately predicted. You'll discover a more in-depth performance profile coupled with a more structured and deliberate assessment will be the key. Start doing this with your next hire, and you won't need to wait until the end of the year for the performance review to provide feedback. Each person will already know how well they're doing. This is what performance management is all about. Using this Performance-based Hiring process, not only will you be hiring more competent and motivated people, you'll also be able to keep them motivated and energized throughout the year.

Strategy, Quality of Hire, and Raising the Talent Bar

This book is not about how to develop a talent acquisition strategy. It's a book about tactics and what it takes to implement a talent acquisition strategy designed to find and hire the top 25%. It doesn't take much of a leap to suggest that Performance-based Hiring can be the means to both implement and measure a company's Raising the Talent Bar strategy. This means implementing processes, procedures, and programs that ensure that the new people hired improve the overall talent level of the company's current workforce. Yet, as described throughout this book, the processes currently used by most companies actually prevent this from happening.

While typical interviewing and assessment tools can differentiate between above and below average performance, they don't do too well in determining whether someone is a Level 3, 4, or 5. Traditional job descriptions are part of the problem, not the solution, since they emphasize skills rather than performance. Generic competency models are similarly flawed, since they don't adjust for the actual job requirements nor any unusual circumstances involved with the actual job. Behavioral interviewing works to some degree by adding structure to the interview and reducing emotional bias, but is not specific enough in measuring variations in good performance. While these tools are adequate for separating the good from the bad, they're far less effective for measuring Quality of Hire.

To more precisely measure pre-hire Quality of Hire, it's essential to understand what drives actual performance and what causes underperformance. Assuming the person hired was appropriate on all traditional measures, a determination then needs to be made as to whether the person was hired for the right job, for the right manager, for the right company, and under the right circumstances. Each factor on the Talent Scorecard provides the information needed to make this determination.

Lack of some type of effective Quality of Hire metric makes implementing a Raising the Talent Bar strategy more difficult since it's hard to know how well the process is working in real time. Most measures currently used for measuring quality are ineffective from a process control standpoint since they're historical. Assessment tests, ranking qualifications, and the use of mini-performance reviews are too late or subject to too many variables to understand where the underlying process is faulty.

The use of the Talent Scorecard provides a practical means to measure and track Quality of Hire. Since the candidate has been assessed in comparison to predicted real job needs, the person can be reassessed throughout the year to see the predicted vs. actual comparison on all the factors in the hiring formula. This is an essential component for any basic process control system. Tracking each score and the overall trends in comparison to current quality levels provides management a means to see if its Raising the Talent Bar program is working. One type of graphical tracking system is shown in the diagram. From this type of dashboard one can imagine zeroing in on specific jobs, and individual managers and recruiters to see if the problems are local or more companywide.

USE METRICS TO MAXIMIZE QUALITY OF HIRE

Improving a process starts by knowing what needs to be improved.

In this example, actual performance is fairly close to predicted for five of the eight factors in the hiring formula. Thinking and Management skills vary the most. The person turned out to be far better at problem-solving than first predicted, but was marginal when it came to managing, planning, and organizing. Actual Managerial Fit dropped also from what was predicted, either due to the manager not being honest about the types of people he or she likes to supervise, or more likely, this critical factor was not assessed.

While real-time feedback is essential for process control, diagnostic metrics like the example shown are needed for process improvement. Once on the job, new hire performance can be tracked at regular intervals to see how predicted performance on any of the factors compares to actual performance. Differences can then be tracked back to problems with interviewing or changes in job requirements and further isolated to individual managers, recruiters, specific jobs, or work locations. Collectively this provides companies a powerful information set to help control who gets hired and how it is done.

The Impact of Talent Scarcity vs. Surplus

It's far easier to find top people when the supply of great talent is greater than the demand. This is rare, especially in technical positions or critical management and staff positions. Yet most companies insist on using a talent surplus approach in a talent scarcity situation. For example, what's the reason companies insist on using traditional job descriptions to attract and subsequently screen out unqualified candidates, when the best candidates don't read them, and they wouldn't apply if they did?

AN ALL TOO-COMMON HR APPROACH FOR IMPROVING QUALITY OF HIRE

Recruiting Needs to Take Companywide Responsibility for Driving Quality of Hire Improvement

I had a recruiter for a well-known and highly respected company at one of our training programs who insisted she would get more unqualified people if she didn't use these skills-based job postings. She already got hundreds from them and she didn't want any more. Even though she got very few good people with these descriptions, this was better than getting more resumes from unqualified people. She obviously didn't see the obvious – they don't work for either keeping out the weak or attracting the best. The associated graphic aptly describes the analytical approach she used to maintain the status quo.

The point of all of this is to suggest that career-focused advertising pushed to a target audience will attract more of the people you want to hire, and fewer of those you don't want to hire. You might need to add a two-step filter as part of this if you somehow attract too many unqualified people. Adding an automatic email response and asking all those who apply to submit a short summary of something they've accomplished related to actual job needs will allow you to quickly separate the qualified from the unqualified.

Reviewing the General Formula for Hiring Success

Throughout this book, and in the studies cited, most problems with hiring, retention, job-satisfaction, and on-the-job performance can be directly tied to lack of situational fit. No matter how talented and capable, if the candidate doesn't fit with the job, the manager, the team, or the company, the person will underperform. Ignoring these issues is at the root cause of just about every bad hiring decision. It also provides the basis for a solution: the hiring formula for success.

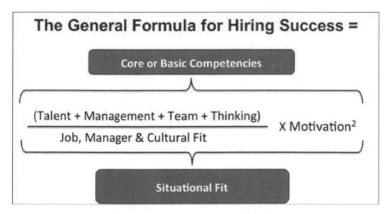

The General Formula for Hiring Success =

Core or Basic Competencies

$$\frac{(\text{Talent} + \text{Management} + \text{Team} + \text{Thinking})}{\text{Job, Manager \& Cultural Fit}} \times \text{Motivation}^2$$

Situational Fit

Situational Fit Drives On-the-Job Performance and Success

The idea is that while a person needs to possess the core traits in abundance, these must all be assessed in relationship to the situational fit factors – the job, manager, team, and company culture. Collectively these drive on-the-job performance, satisfaction, and motivation. Motivation is clearly the most important factor in the equation, but its source is the situational fit factors. No matter how inherently self-motivated a person is, it's not worth much if the fit is wrong. This is the real value of the performance profile – not only does it clarify job expectations, it also captures all of the essential fit factors.

Process Control and Metrics

Companies that have implemented Performance-based Hiring start by preparing performance profiles for a few jobs and then work through the rest of the sourcing, interviewing, and recruiting process to get the kinks out before scaling it companywide. In its simplest form, new job requisitions need to include a performance profile with everyone on the hiring team in agreement including, and especially, the recruiter assigned with the task of finding passive candidates.

PROCESS IMPROVEMENT STARTS BY MEASURING THE PROCESS

+ or - .5

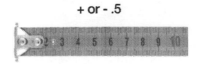

Scorecard Variance

Require Narrow Difference Among the Interview Team Members

Before a yes/no hiring decision is made, a formal debriefing based on the sharing of evidence is required. A key condition of this is that there can be no more than a plus or minus half a point difference on any of the factors in the Talent Scorecard among the hiring team interviewers. This is typically what occurs when actual evidence is shared. It's much wider than this when emotions, intuition, or feelings are the basis of the assessment. The "plus or minus .5" rule is a good way to control the natural tendency for interviewers to make quick superficial judgments about candidates based on little evidence. This is Process Control 101: wide variances indicate a process out of control and tight variances indicate a process in control.

Is Your Hiring Process Broken?

If you need to see more than four candidates for any job, stop seeing more candidates.

Track Interviews per Hire to Control the Entire Process

One of my favorite metrics, and quite frankly one of the most important, is interviews per hire. This metric provides a quick snapshot of how any individual search is going. If a hiring manager needs to see too many candidates there's obviously something wrong. I consider four as a good target. If it takes more than four candidates to be seen before a person is hired, something is either fundamentally wrong with the hiring process, or the skill level of those involved making the yes/no decisions is suspect. To further prevent wasted effort, stop the process if someone isn't hired by the time the fourth candidate is presented. When you do, you'll discover the likely cause to be one of the following big issues:

Top Ten Reasons Why Most Managers Need to See More than Four Candidates to Make a Hire

1) They're not seeing enough top candidates, so the manager is waiting for the ideal person to magically appear.

2) The hiring manager is not fully engaged or lacks the leadership skills needed to attract and build a world-class team.

3) Recruiters aren't able to convince passive candidates to at least entertain an exploratory conversation with the hiring manager about the career merits of the opportunity.

4) Lack of consensus among the interviewing team regarding candidate competence and suitability. This is typically due to a variety of different and flawed interviewing techniques being used.

5) Lack of a common understanding of real job needs by those on the hiring team, including recruiters, sourcers, the hiring manager, and other interviewers.

6) Using a talent surplus hiring process, i.e., screening out the weak when a talent scarcity condition actually exists.

7) If the compensation is in the top-third for comparable positions, the problem with hiring top people is typically an inability to close due to weak negotiating and recruiting skills.

8) Too much focus on Before Year 1, Day 1, and Moment 1 when top talent is primarily interested in Year 1 and Beyond.

9) Lack of a true partnership between the hiring manager and the recruiter/sourcer. Everyone needs to be on the same page from beginning to end.

10) Recruiters don't have the time or resources to do what it takes to hire top talent.

This book was written to address every one of these problems. Bottom line, it takes a rethinking of the hiring strategy and each step in the process to implement it properly. While getting to four interviews per hire is no easy task, it's not impossible, and as a minimum, it's a worthy process improvement target. Note: if you're hiring lots of the same people (e.g., sales reps for the same job), the candidates-to-hire ratio should be no more than two to three!

From a practical standpoint, hiring managers have to take the lead on the whole process. Don't delegate it to HR. Instead, if you're a hiring manager own it yourself. Be fully engaged and fully responsible. And if you need to see more than four people to hire a great person to raise your department's talent level, look at yourself first – you're probably the problem – before blaming others.

Regardless, if you're a hiring manager don't compromise your hiring standards. Everyone you hire represents your personal future, and in the end, don't sacrifice this future by making short-term decisions for the sake of expediency.

Summary – Implementing Performance-based Hiring

- **Align strategy, tactics, process, and people.** Hiring top people takes more than just finding and interviewing them. Hiring the best people in a talent-scarcity situation at a minimum requires great jobs, strong recruiters, and managers who are fully invested in hiring top people. Strong metrics are required in order to ensure that best practices and processes are used correctly and consistently, but most important of all is a talent acquisition strategy that is more than just talk.

- **Don't use short-term information to make long-term decisions.** Companies, recruiters, hiring managers, and candidates alike often miss the forest for the trees. Finding the best person who applies to fill an open requisition is not the same as hiring a top person who's looking to make a career move. Screen on performance and potential rather than on skills, experience, and compensation. If you're looking for a job, don't ask about the compensation, ask about the challenges involved in the job and the long-term opportunity if successful.

- **Use performance profiles to become a better manager.** Use performance profiles rather than job descriptions for assessment, onboarding, and performance management. Remember, it's what people do with what they have that makes them successful. Clarifying expectations upfront is the number one driver of performance and job satisfaction. Assess and hire people the same way you promote them.

- **Use Performance-based Hiring to implement a "Raising the Talent Bar" program.** Hiring top people on a consistent basis requires a fully integrated approach that links sourcing, assessment, and recruiting into a tightly integrated process. This is what Performance-based Hiring is all about. However, it's not enough to raise a company's talent level. This requires a means to ensure that every hiring decision meets the company's long-term talent objectives, not just the hiring manager's short-term need to fill a seat with the best person who shows up.

- **Use the talent scorecard to measure and track Quality of Hire.** The talent scorecard provides a means to measure pre-hire Quality of Hire by assessing comparable performance against real job needs. As long as job needs haven't shifted much, this same method can be used to measure actual on-the-job Quality of Hire. Actual vs. predicted performance can then be used to improve the interviewing and assessment process.

- **Use the Hiring Formula for Success to measure situational fit.** The primary reason otherwise talented people underperform is lack of motivation to do the work, a clash of styles with the hiring manager, or misalignment on company culture and values. It's essential that these situational fit factors be considered in a formal and deliberate way to maximize performance, job satisfaction, and retention.

- **Stop if you need to see more than four candidates to make a hiring decision.** There is something fundamentally wrong with a company's hiring process if hiring managers need to see more than four candidates for any opening. Typically problems are attributed to lack of understanding of real job needs, weak interviewing skills, bad recruitment advertising, or a process focused on weeding out the weak, rather than attracting the best. It's best to rethink the process rather than hope a great person will eventually show up who has an economic need to apply, is a high achiever, and is willing to take a lateral transfer. This is typically an unnecessary and very long wait.

Afterword

It's pretty obvious that you can't use a talent surplus approach for finding top talent when a talent surplus doesn't exist. Yet despite the evidence, too many companies still try. It makes little sense to continue to post skills-infested job descriptions and weeding out the weak with the hope that a few good people remain at the end.

In a talent scarcity situation when the demand for talent outstrips the supply, a company's talent acquisition effort needs to be designed to attract and nurture the best. This requires the development of compelling career-oriented jobs, engaged hiring managers, and highly skilled recruiters. By focusing on performance rather than skills and experience, not only will a company be able to hire more highly qualified people, but it will also be able to open up its talent pool to more diverse candidates, more high-potential candidates with a different mix of skills & experiences, and more great returning military veterans who deserve great jobs. Collectively, this is what *The Essential Guide for Hiring & Getting Hired* is about.

Hiring the best talent is not just about better interviewing skills, although this is a part of it. It's also not about better sourcing, networking and recruitment advertising, although these are all critical parts. It's also not just about better recruiting and negotiating skills, although they're both critical since you can't afford to lose good people for the wrong reasons. Hiring the best talent is about having the right talent acquisition strategy, a fully-integrated hiring process based on how top people get jobs, and a fully committed management team that believes hiring great people is how you build great companies. That's what is meant when people say hiring top people is the most important thing every manager needs to do.

If you're a job-seeker, this book will not help you get a job you don't deserve, but by knowing how you'll be found, assessed and hired, it will help you get one you do.

Talent Rules! It's about time.

Appendix

1) General Validation of Performance-based Hiring by David Goldstein, Shareholder, Littler Mendelson. Email info@louadlergroup.com to review the complete white paper.

2) The Two-Question Performance-based Interview

3) Quality of Hire Talent Scorecard

4) Ideal Candidate Persona and Profile

5) Candidate Decision-making and Job Comparison Matrix

Important Notice on Obtaining and Using PDF Versions of these Forms

A complete full-size set of these forms is available for the purchaser of this book by completing our online form (http://budurl.com/AGEGFH). We'll be holding frequent complimentary webcasts for job-seekers, hiring managers, recruiters, and business leaders on how to apply the concepts presented in *The Essential Guide for Hiring & Getting Hired*. After completing the form, and agreeing to the usage terms below, you'll need to use this password to open the documents: EGFH2013

PERFORMANCE-BASED HIRING AND LEGAL COMPLIANCE OVERVIEW

DAVID J. GOLDSTEIN*

Businesses hire people because there is a job to be done. The goal is to find the right people, bring them on board, and get them to work. When the wrong person is hired, the work doesn't get done. Worse yet, the productivity of others may be disrupted. And in the worst case a bad hire can lead to litigation. Employment related litigation is extremely costly and legal fees represent just the tip of the iceberg. Litigation distracts managers, impacts employee morale, and often breeds additional litigation.

For these and other reasons, successful companies need to adopt an effective approach to recruiting and hiring. Performance-based Hiring provides such an approach.

By creating compelling job descriptions that are focused on key performance objectives, using advanced marketing and networking concepts to find top people, by adopting evidence-based interviewing techniques, and by integrating recruiting into the interviewing process, companies can attract better candidates and make better hiring decisions.

Because the Performance-based Hiring system does differ from traditional recruiting and hiring processes, questions arise as to whether employers can adopt Performance-based Hiring and still comply with the complex array of statutes, regulations, and common law principals that regulate the workplace. The answer is yes.

In particular:

- A properly prepared performance profile can identify and document the essential functions of a job better than traditional position descriptions, facilitating the reasonable accommodation of disabilities and making it easier to comply with the Americans with Disabilities Act and similar laws.

• Even employers that maintain more traditional job descriptions may still use performance profiles or summaries of performance profiles to advertise job openings. Employers are not legally required to post their internal job descriptions when advertising an open position. Nor is there any legal obligation to (or advantage in) posting boring ads.

• Under some circumstances, federal government contractors will want to include in their job postings, objective, non-comparative qualifications for the position to be filled. Using SMARTe, employers can create performance-based job descriptions that include such objective, non-comparative elements. Requiring applicants to have previously accomplished specific tasks represents a selection criterion that is no less objective than requiring years of experience in some general area.

• Focusing on "Year 1 and Beyond" criteria may open the door to more minority, military, and disabled candidates who have a less "traditional" mix of experiences, thereby supporting affirmative action or diversity efforts.

• The law permits employers to define who will be an "applicant" by limiting consideration to individuals who fulfill certain procedural requirements such as fully completing an application form. Requiring interested individuals to complete a short write-up of some accomplishment related to the job to be filled (the "two-step") can serve as such a requirement. Individuals who do not submit the required write-up need not be considered as applicants for record-keeping purposes. Of course, while individuals can be rejected based on the quality of their submission, those individuals who do submit the write-up will need to be counted as applicants.

- Conducting performance-based interviews ensures that the interviews will be structured and properly focused, and minimizes the risk of an interviewer inquiring into protected characteristics. Moreover, since the performance-based interviews are conducted pursuant to a common methodology, one is assured that the candidates are being fairly compared.

- Performance-based interviewing promotes fair consideration of the different skills and experiences that each candidate has to offer – which is essential to promoting diversity.

- One obstacle to diversity in hiring is the greater effort required for an interviewer to connect with a person who is different. The Essential Guide for Hiring & Getting Hired offers techniques for controlling this type of bias. Waiting 30 minutes and using the Plus or Minus Reversal Technique will reduce the impact of such biases and promote greater diversity in hiring.

- Although some employers may be required to maintain records of the actual applicant pools considered for each hire, a single posting may still be used to cover multiple openings by narrowing the pool through the two-step process and maintaining appropriate applicant tracking systems.

- Performance-based Hiring is a business process for hiring top talent. While the process will be useful for filling many different types of jobs, there may be some jobs (for example, lower level, lower skilled, high turnover positions) for which it doesn't make sense to use Performance-based Hiring. That is not a problem. Employers need to be consistent in their hiring processes for similar positions, but remain free to adopt different processes for different positions.

˙David J. Goldstein, a shareholder in Littler Mendelson's Minneapolis office, has over 25 years of experience working with in-house counsel, business leadership, and HR professionals to proactively identify and implement creative solutions for complying with legal and regulatory requirements, avoiding liability, and resolving internal and external disputes.

An experienced trial lawyer, David's clients include health care providers, construction companies, financial institutions, colleges and universities, and professional sports teams. David devotes a significant portion of his practice to assisting employers with the implementation and maintenance of effective affirmative action programs and representing contractors before the OFCCP.

David has a J.D. from Harvard Law School and a B.A. from Haverford College. While in law school he also taught freshman economics at Harvard College. Additional information on David is available at http://www.linkedin.com/in/davidjgoldstein and http://www.littler. com/people/david-j-goldstein

THE PERFORMANCE-BASED INTERVIEW

Lou Adler's Performance-based Interview
October 2012

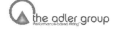
the adler group
Performance-based Hiring™

Note: This interview is based on Lou Adler's two books, *Hire With Your Head* and *The Essential Guide for Hiring & Getting Hired*, and should be used in conjunction with the **Quality of Hire Talent Scorecard**. Obtain examples for each performance objective in the performance profile before making a final decision. Wait at least 30 minutes before making any yes/no decision. Measure first impression AFTER YOU DETERMINE COMPETENCY to increase assessment accuracy dramatically.

Step 1	Welcome and Review Job/Motivation	Information & Hot Tips
Opening question to determine job-hunting status and motivation for looking for a job	Provide a 1-2 minute overview of the job, or ask if the person needs more information about the general content of the job. Then ask: *What are you looking for in a new job?* (pause) *Why is having ____ and ____ important to you, and why do you think this job meets those criteria?*	Find out what's already been covered. This way you'll be able to focus your questions and fact-finding. Asking the "Why?" follow-up question allows you to understand the person's reasons for looking and what the person would require in a new position.

Step 2	Bring Impact of First Impressions to Conscious Level	Information & Hot Tips
Action: be aware of your biases	Write down your immediate emotional reaction to the candidate – relaxed, uptight, or neutral. Write down the cause. At the end of the interview you'll measure your first impression of the candidate again, when you're less affected by it. Determine objectively how your first impression would help or hinder on-the-job performance.	o Wait 30 minutes o Do opposite of normal reaction o Like: prove incompetency, be tough o Dislike: prove competency, be easy o Ask same questions to all o Be cynical, get proof, examples, facts

Step 3	Review Work History and Achiever Pattern	Fact-finding & Hot Tips
Use this to develop structure behind experience and accomplishments Look for "Achiever Pattern"	*Please tell me about your most recent job. What was your position, the company, your duties, and any recognition you received?* (Do this for the past few jobs.) For students or younger candidates: *Tell me about your schooling and advanced training.* (Look for special studies, awards, going the extra mile, self-development.) Spend 15-20 minutes on this. For each position obtain: title, promotions, basic duties, 360° team chart, impact made, challenges faced, any recognition received. Go back 5-10 years looking for upward trend of growth. Ask why the person changed jobs, looking for a career growth decision pattern. If the person is an achiever, but growth has stalled, or the current job is not highly satisfying, your job might be a good move.	Look for basic fit and Achiever Pattern. **Achiever Pattern:** o Faster growth, more promotions o Special awards, bonuses, raises o Assigned to bigger projects o Offered special education o Hired or pushed by mentor **Look for career opportunity gaps** o Differences in scope and span o More important projects o Broader influence and exposure o Faster growth

Step 4	Most Significant Accomplishment Question (MSA)	Fact-finding & Hot Tips
Ask the MSA question for all performance objectives in the performance profile	*Can you please tell me about a major one-time project or accomplishment? Or, consider a project or event that you're quite proud of.* *One major project we're now working on is* (describe). *Please tell me about something comparable you've worked on.* Spend 10-12 minutes on 2-3 major accomplishments in order to develop a trend line of accomplishments over time. Make note of the accomplishments and type of work where the person excelled and/or was highly motivated to exceed expectations.	o Overview of job, company o Team and org structure o Environment – pace, resources o When? How long? Results? o What results were expected? o Walk through plan and results o What would you do differently? o Describe tech skills and how applied o Learn what tech skills and how used o Obtain 2-3 examples of initiative o What did you change/improve? o Describe biggest problem solved o Walk through biggest decision made o Describe likes, dislikes o Where did you exceed expectations? o How did you improve yourself? o What would you do differently? o What recognition did you receive?

Lou Adler's Performance-based Interview

October 2012

Step 4a	Team Version of MSA Question	Fact-finding & Hot Tips
Question for few teams & observe impact and trend line	*Can you please tell me about a major team accomplishment? Consider one where you led the team, and one where you were a key member of the team.* Spend 10-12 minutes on 1-2 team accomplishments. Observe trend line and changes in scope of team. Make note of the types of people on the team, variety of functions worked with, and how influential the person was in changing the direction of the team.	o Prepare 360° work chart with titles o What was your role, why you? o What was plan & were results met? o What were biggest team problems? o How did you influence results? o 3 examples of initiative helping others o Examples of being influenced o How could you have been better? o Describe biggest conflict & resolution o Examples coaching others o Examples of being coached o Did you receive any team recognition?

Step 5	Problem Solving Question (PSQ)	Fact-finding & Hot Tips
Repeat question 1-2 times using real problems Anchor with MSA question	*One major problem we're now facing is _____. How would you go about addressing this? What would you need to know, and how would you plan it out?* *What have you done that's most similar?* (This is an Anchor to insure that the candidate doesn't just talk a good game. This might have been covered above.)	o What would you need to know? o What would you do first, why? o Who else would you involve? o How would you plan, organize effort? o How would you prioritize tasks, why? o How would you find out critical issues o How would you figure out resources o How long would it take, why? o What would you do if...? o How would you make this trade-off? o How would you make business case?

Step 6	Let the Candidate Ask Questions	Fact-finding & Hot Tips
Tell candidates they can ask questions at the end	*Based on what we've discussed so far, do you have any questions?* It's important to delay candidate questions until the end. Meaningful questions at the end of the interview are insightful, since they demonstrate that the candidate has processed all she/he has heard so far.	o Evaluate if the questions were meaningful, appropriate, and relevant o Determine if the candidate is focusing on the long-term career opportunity or just short-term issues

Step 7	Determine Interest and Recruit	Fact-finding & Hot Tips
Question & Discussion Create Job Stretch	*While I've seen a few other very strong candidates, I'm also impressed with some of the work you've done. What are your thoughts now about this job? Is this something you'd like to consider further? Why? Why not?* Only the hiring manager and recruiter need to ask this. Others can ask a softer variation (e.g., "What are your thoughts about the job?")	o State sincere interest o Make candidate earn job o Listen 4x more than talk; don't sell o Describe concerns to create gap o Mention other strong contenders o What other jobs are you considering? o How interested on 1-10 scale, why? o What's needed to know to get to 8-9? o Link job to big company projects o What do you like/dislike? o How does job meets your needs? o Compensation needs, availability o When can you come back, next steps

Step 8	Measure First Impression Again	Information & Hot Tips
Compare candidate's true personality to 1st impression at opening of interview	Measure first impression again at the end of the interview. Consider the actual impact on you, the actual impact on others (customers, peers, superiors, staff), and the actual impact of personality and style on performance.	o Did candidate get better or worse? o Become more/less nervous? o Open up more, talk more? o Did you observe true personality in accomplishments? o Were your biases controlled? o Did this change your decision? o Is true personality consistent with job needs?

QUALITY OF HIRE TALENT SCORECARD

Quality of Hire Talent Scorecard
Based on Lou Adler's *The Essential Guide for Hiring & Getting Hired*

Candidate: _____ Position: _____ Interviewer: _____ Date: _____

Factor	Level 1 Minimal	Level 2 Adequate	2.5 Average	Level 3 Strong	Level 4 Great	Level 5 Superb	Rank
BASIC FIT FACTORS							
Skills	Bare minimum.	Has the basics, but needs help.	Covers all direct job needs well.		Extremely strong in all job needs.	Brings far more to table.	
Experience	Minimum threshold.	Meets most, but not all needs.	Meets all experience needs.		Broader experience.	Perfect fit plus more.	
Achiever Pattern	No evidence the person is in the top 50%.	Some, but not sure if person is in top 50%.	Evidence clearly indicates person is top 25%!		Evidence clearly indicates person is in top 10-15%.	Evidence clearly indicates person is in top 5%.	
CORE COMPETENCIES							
Talent	Meets bare minimum standards. Needs too much support.	Can do the work, but needs added training, support.	Technically tops. An asset. Can learn quickly. Covers it all.		Top-notch. Trains others. Constantly improving. Brings more to the table.	Brilliant. Sets standards. Leader in field. Sought out. Recognized.	
Management	Unorganized. Very reactive. Misses most deadlines.	Needs direction, monitoring. More reactive than plan.	Solid planner, organizer. Executes well. Anticipates issues.		Excellent. Plans, anticipates, communicates, and succeeds.	Handles complex projects. Makes it happen. Anticipates everything.	
Team	Little team growth. Limited examples of leading or influencing others.	Some team growth, but needs urging. Okay examples of influencing others.	Good team growth. Has taken on bigger team roles.		Clear team track. Takes initiative to help others. Takes lead.	Impressive team growth. Persuades, motivates, coaches. Asked to lead.	
Thinking	Didn't understand any key issues or develop any solutions.	Understood most issues, developed okay solutions.	Clearly understood all key issues and developed very well.		Understood all key & less obvious issues. Works w/ others. Developed multiple solutions.	Seeks best solutions. Understood core issues & provides new insights.	
SITUATIONAL FIT FACTORS							
Job Fit	Limited comparability with accomplishments and job needs.	Some comparable accomplishments, but limited or inconsistent.	Accomplishments clearly comparable with consistent results.		Achieved better results doing similar work in similar environments.	Full job match with exceptional results – scope, pace, resources.	
Managerial Fit	Mismatch between candidate's & manager's style.	Limited, but has worked with similar managers.	Successfully worked with similar managers.		Person easily adapts to a variety of manager styles	Super fit. Coaches upward. Both are flexible.	
Culture & Environment	Complete mismatch on culture & environment.	Reasonable match on culture and environment.	Close match on culture and environment.		Excellent match and has made similar transfers.	Thrives in this type of environment, culture.	
Motivation[2]	Very limited evidence of motivation to do this type of work.	Will do the work, but needs extra pushing.	Self-motivated to do this type of work w/ normal supervision.		Takes initiative to do more, faster, & better. Self improves in this type of work.	Totally committed to do whatever it takes to get it done. Constant self-development.	
OVERALL FIT							
Notes:							

CANDIDATE PERSONA

the adler group

Top Performer Job-hunter Persona/Profile

Position: _____

The following table allows you to gain some important insight into your ideal candidate. You'll use this information to prepare recruitment advertising messages (postings, emails, voice mails) and for developing active and passive candidate sourcing programs. The form should be used in conjunction with Lou Adler's two books, *Hire With Your Head* and *The Essential Guide for Hiring & Getting Hired*.

Key Factors to Consider	Comments	Ideas and Comments
What is candidate looking for in a new job?	Career move, a better job, or a lateral transfer.	
What is causing ideal candidate to look or leave current job?	Active vs. Passive. Are person's going-away reasons stronger than their going-towards?	
What phase of job-hunting process is ideal candidate likely to be in?	Explorer, Tiptoer, Googler, Networker, Hunter, Talent Pool.	
Types of jobs previously held	Consider growth of candidate position to position. Rate of change is important.	
Build 360° network	Who would have worked with the candidate? These are great for warm referrals.	
Direct & functional competitors	Consider vendors or non-competitive firms, or specialist organizations.	
Comparative titles	Consider every type of title imaginable. Be generic in your ads!	
Candidate SEO terms	What terms would a candidate use to Google for the job?	
Recognition and Achiever terms	Consider awards & recognition likely for this type of person.	
Professional societies & groups	What groups does the person join on LinkedIn? Is the person a member of yours?	
Demographic or diversity terms	Consider special groups or keywords.	
Personal advisory team	Who will help person decide, and what info do they need?	
Primary selection criteria	What factors will they use to compare positions?	
Primary underlying intrinsic motivator	What is the primary factor driving person to consider another opportunity?	

CANDIDATE DECISION MATRIX

The Candidate Offer Comparison and Decision-Making Process

How to use this form: This form allows a candidate to objectively compare different job opportunities. It's based on Lou Adler's two books, *Hire With Your Head* and *The Essential Guide for Hiring & Getting Hired*. The key point is to examine all of the short- and long-term factors in balance rather than emphasizing compensation and location. Emphasizing Year One and Beyond criteria will maximize career growth. Don't allow desperation or convenience to dominate the decision-making.

Career Strategy	Decision Stage	Primary Criteria	New Opportunity	Current Position	Other Options	Comments
Compensation Maximization	**Day One Criteria**	Compensation				
		Location				
		Company				
		Job Title				
		Other				
		BRIDGING THE GAP				
	Year One Criteria	Real job focus				
		Impact, visibility				
		Challenge				
		Hiring manager				
		Hiring team				
		Company culture				
		Learning				
		Job stretch				
		Work/Life balance				
		Comp/Benefits				
		Key circumstances				
		Other				
Career Growth Maximization	**Beyond Year One Criteria**	Growth opportunity				
		Hiring manager				
		Mentors/Leaders				
		Company issues				
		Business conditions				
		Key circumstances				
		Total Rewards				
		Other				

the adler group

LINKS

The shortened links used throughout the book are expanded here for your convenience & future reference.

Introduction

1   http://talent.linkedin.com/blog/index.php/2011/12/passive-candidates-accelerate/
2   http://www.nytimes.com/2011/03/13/business/13hire.html

Chapter 1

3   http://www.youtube.com/watch?v=G0FpjxRg4cM

Chapter 4

4   http://en.wikipedia.org/wiki/Maslow's_hierarchy_of_needs

Chapter 6

5   http://louadlergroup.com/links/job-description-li-ad-sample/
6   http://louadlergroup.com/why-you-must-eliminate-job-descriptions/

Chapter 7

7   http://louadlergroup.com/training/recruiter-boot-camp-online/
8   http://business.linkedin.com/talent-solutions/products.html#recruiter

Chapter 8

9   http://www.careerbuilder.com/JobPoster/Products/page.aspx?pagever=SupplyDemandPortal
10 http://talent.linkedin.com/blog/index.php/2012/10/talent-pools/
11 https://support.google.com/websearch/bin/answer.py?hl=en&answer=136861
12 http://hbcuconnect.com/colleges/
13 http://www.nsbe.org
14 http://www.nshmba.org/page/Splash_Page/
15 http://www.egrabber.com/louadler/ldg/
16 http://louadlergroup.com/training/
17 http://www.businessinsider.com/7-cool-resumes-we-found-on-pinterest-2012-2

Chapter 10

18 http://www.linkedin.com/today/post/article/20121020150801-15454-use-solution-selling-to-ace-the-interview

19 http://www.glassdoor.com/blog/top-25-oddball-interview-questions-2011/

Chapter 11

20 http://www.youtube.com/watch?v=G0FpjxRg4cM

21 http://home.ncifcrf.gov/SAICFTraining/2011_Gallup_Questions.pdf

22 http://www.nytimes.com/2011/03/13/business/13hire.html

Appendix

23 http://louadlergroup.com/articles/essential-guide-hiring-getting-hired/

ABOUT THE AUTHOR

Lou Adler is the president of The Adler Group (louadlergroup.com), an international training and consulting firm helping companies implement Performance-based Hiring. He is the Amazon bestselling author of *Hire With Your Head* (John Wiley & Sons, 3rd Edition, 2007), the Nightingale-Conant audio program *Talent Rules! Using Performance-based Hiring to Hire Top Talent* (2007) and *The Essential Guide for Hiring & Getting Hired* (Workbench 2013). Adler is a noted recruiting industry expert, international speaker, and columnist for a number of major recruiting and HR organization sites including SHRM, HRPA, SMA, ERE, LinkedIn, Kennedy Information and HR.com. He holds an MBA from UCLA and a BS in Engineering from Clarkson University.

The Essential Guide for Hiring & Getting Hired

by Lou Adler

ALSO AVAILABLE AS AN EBOOK FROM THESE BOOKSELLERS:

Amazon   Barnes & Noble   iBooks   Kobo

visit HireAndGetHired.com

WORKBENCH MEDIA